Congratulations on completing 55

FOR WOMEN

Refresh

Refresh

19 WAYS TO BOOST YOUR SPIRITUAL LIFE

BY RON HUGHES

Refresh: 19 Ways to Boost Your Spiritual Life
By: Ron Hughes
Copyright © 2011
GOSPEL FOLIO PRESS
All Rights Reserved

This book or parts thereof may not be reproduced in any form, stored in a retrieval system, or transmitted in any form by any means – electronic, mechanical, photocopy, recording, or otherwise – without prior written permission of the publisher except as provided by Canadian copyright law.

Published by
GOSPEL FOLIO PRESS
304 Killaly St. W.
Port Colborne, ON L3K 6A6
CANADA

ISBN: 9781926765495

Cover design by Lisa Martin

Scripture quotations marked (ESV) are from The Holy Bible, English Standard Version® (ESV®) Copyright © 2001 by Crossway, a publishing ministry of Good News Publishers. All rights reserved. ESV Text Edition: 2007

Scripture quotations marked (NIV) are taken from the Holy Bible, New International Version®, NIV®. Copyright © 1973, 1978, 1984 by Biblica, Inc.™ Used by permission of Zondervan. All rights reserved worldwide. www.zondervan.com

Scripture quotations marked (NKJV™) are taken from the New King James Version®. Copyright © 1982 by Thomas Nelson, Inc. Used by permission. All rights reserved.

Internet addresses printed in this book are offered as a resource and are not intended to be or imply an endorsement by the author or the publisher, nor do we vouch for the content of these sites for the life of this book.

Printed in USA

What people are saying about: *Refresh*

"Basing his thoughts on refreshingly told Bible stories, Ron Hughes has called us back to the basics of a walk with God. He accomplishes this by reflecting on many of the 'old' spiritual disciplines and bringing some 'less-thought-of-ones' to the fore. Though his '19 ways' are actions, they focus more on the heart of a God-follower who wants to have an intimate relationship with his Creator. A joy to read, a challenge to do and a privilege to experience."

Jim Allen, Global Pastor, HCJB Global

"I found Ron's book to be inspiring, encouraging and motivating, and his writing style especially easy to follow. This is a book for ordinary people who desire to become extraordinary by being more like Jesus, and I highly recommend it. It is one that should be in every home, church, and library."

Sue Augustine, best-selling author and international motivational speaker for 25 years and owner of Sue Augustine Seminars

"This book is just what many of us need. Ron Hughes speaks simply and deeply of the realities of cultivating our walk with God. This book is refreshing and clear, like pure, cool water on a hot day. If you're thirsty to go deeper with God, I warmly commend this work to you."

Gregg Harris, President, Far East Broadcasting Company

"This is an important, practical and unique book, that will, if you work through the 19 ways to boost your spiritual life, make a huge difference to the way you enjoy your life in Christ. From getting started, to enjoying rest in Christ, this book, with its interesting take on biblical stories and its practical applications could make a significant difference to your life. I am happy to recommend it with enthusiasm."

Dr. David Humphreys, Emeritus Professor, McMaster University, Canada

"Ron's approach to teaching truths of Scripture is both practical and powerful. He openly and honestly challenges his readers with pithy quotes, stories of Bible characters, and with Scripture. Twenty-first century issues are addressed, such as how to find time for God in today's electronically-driven society. This book is a 'must read' for all who desire a deeper relationship with the Lord."

Della Letkeman, author of Ants and Voice in the Darkness

"The life of a disciple of Jesus is not necessarily a life of doing external acts. It is a matter of the inner life, those spiritual disciplines that promote spiritual transformation. They are the 'below the surface things,' things that others will never see or observe, but Jesus does. Jesus is the 'audience of one' who can take the principles and practices that Ron Hughes is talking about and make them resound through all of eternity. Read the book carefully and deeply. These are spiritual secrets that are priceless."

Lauren Libby, President/CEO, TWR International

"Prepare yourself for the journey of your life. En route you will come upon 19 'Rest Stops' strategically placed to invite you to pause in your pursuit of a closer walk with the Lord and a deeper experience of the Christian life. Time spent at each stop, to internalize the practical and pertinent guidance, will not only shorten the journey but make it the adventure of your life."

William J. McRae, President Emeritus,
Tyndale University College & Seminary

"When Jesus becomes our source of hope, a new way of life begins. But it doesn't just happen automatically. Ron's very practical guide to spiritual vitality helps us face some of the challenges we will encounter as we seek to follow Christ. As the pace of life continually increases, we must carve out time to spend in the presence of Christ and grow in His likeness. Ron shows us that our destiny is to be with God Himself. We are journeying towards Him, and when we see Him we shall be like Him—that is our hope."

Hugo Wolmarans, Director Arab World Media,
a ministry of Pioneers

Table of Contents

Dedication & Acknowledgments	9
Foreword	11
Getting Started	13
1. Find Quiet Space for Yourself	17
2. Be Quiet	25
3. Confess Your Faults	33
4. Meditate	41
5. Serve Others	47
6. Pray	53
7. Say "No" to Yourself	59
8. Live Simply	65
9. Sacrifice Yourself	73
10. Be Generous	79
11. Keep Some Secrets	87
12. Be Open	95
13. Connect with Others	103
14. Learn to Submit	111
15. Study Your Bible	119
16. Worship	125
17. Embrace Suffering	131
18. Celebrate Good Things	139
19. Rest	147
Afterword	153
The Stories and Where to Find Them	155
FBH International	157

Dedication

I offer this book with gratitude to members, past and present, of the Board of Directors of FBH International. You have stood with me in the goal of helping people around the world know the Lord Jesus Christ and grow in their relationship with Him.

Acknowledgments

I would like to acknowledge the following friends who have contributed to the production of this book in a variety of ways: Alison Berry, George Berry, Joanne Easby, Jim Howlett, Deborah Piggott, Greg Reader, Hazel Robinson, Don Ruddle and Janice Vardy. Special thanks goes to my wife, Debbie Hughes, for her encouragement.

Foreword

Writing about *19 ways to boost your spiritual life* has two challenges:

- Some people will think the writer practices them faithfully and with great spiritual results. Then, they look at their own efforts and give up.
- Others will think the writer is a big phoney, being sure he doesn't practise all he preaches. They look at him and think that because he falls short, they don't need to try.

I have never met anyone who is satisfied with his or her spiritual life. Every one of us can be more like Jesus. That is what this little book is all about: being more like Jesus.

If you, like me, know you fall far short in that dimension, then "Refresh" is for you. I wrote it for people like us. People who have sometimes tried and failed and sometimes simply never tried.

I encourage you to join me on this journey of spiritual growth. How you approach it is up to you, but I suggest you tackle the ideas one at a time spending as long as necessary to make them part of your life. If all you have done when you are finished reading is to gain a working knowledge of *19 ways you could boost your spiritual life*, we've both failed. If, however, you're even just a little bit more like Jesus, we both have reason to celebrate.

—May 2011

P.S. Visit www.fbhinternational.com to find additional material and a study guide to help you apply what you learn as well as put you in touch with others who are travelling the same road.

Getting Started

God intends for each of us to have a significant, fulfilled life, even if we don't fall into the Moses, Deborah, Paul or Phoebe categories. Because of the global effects of sin, we have obstacles to deal with along the way. These are thrown up by demonic spirits, the world system and our own willful tendencies which are opposed to God and hinder our experiencing the kind of life God intends for us.

A question to get you thinking: Which is the better metaphor for the Christian life—marching or dancing?

In Philippians 3, Paul gives an overview of his spiritual goals: *"Indeed, I count everything as loss because of the surpassing worth of knowing Christ Jesus my Lord. For His sake I have suffered the loss of all things and count them as rubbish, in order that I may gain Christ and be found in him, not having a righteousness of my own that comes from the law, but that which comes through faith in Christ, the righteousness from God that depends on faith—that I may know Him and the power of His resurrection, and may share His sufferings, becoming like Him in His death, that by any means possible I may attain the resurrection from the dead"* (Phil. 3:8-11 ESV).

Observe:

- Knowing Jesus was more than just Paul's first priority—it was his only priority.
- He made this a fact as well as a philosophical position (He suffered loss as well as counted things as loss).
- Being "found in Christ" is a life of faith—not of human effort.
- Paul was committed to knowing Jesus to the point where God's power would be released in his life.

- He was willing to suffer for Jesus, even to becoming like Him in death, that he might participate in the resurrection.

We become like Christ by following Him. The more time we spend in His presence, the more we will be conformed to His likeness.

This is not always a conscious process, though there are conscious aspects. The most profound change happens in our spirit where God's Spirit works without our active participation.

For years I played piano. While never attaining more than modest ability, I did discover that some pieces cannot be played immediately. Their technical demands prevent one from mastering them by simply practising the piece itself. The aspiring musician must spend time working on scales, exercises and studies first. All of this work on technique prepares one to eventually be able to play the piece.

Just as Jesus humbled Himself to be baptized, though He had no need for repentance, He modelled many of the things I'll be covering in this book, though His relationship with the Father was such that it did not need improvement. His disciples and, later, the early church followed His example and teaching regarding these activities which deepened their relationship with the Father. When we engage in these same activities our relationship with God will likewise be deepened.

As we start, we need to ask ourselves if we want to change this way. Some will be eager to sign on. Others, not interested when first confronted with the idea, may be open to being persuaded to engage actively in their development. Sadly, we can identify a final category consisting of those who dig in and resist spiritual change because the personal price seems too high.

Embracing these practices to deepen your spiritual life will disrupt it. Not only will they affect how you spend your resources (time, energy, talent, money and so on), they will impinge on your personality as they gradually affect how you respond in attitude, word and action to people and situations.

At the same time, these practices will not rob you of your personality, though they will filter out the sinful expressions of it which are so natural, so normal, so ingrained. While we are looking for positive change, it is possible that the pursuit of these practices will make us disciples of the Pharisees rather than of the Lord Jesus. We need to be alert to the danger of becoming legalistic in our commitment to them.

Any gardener will tell you that preparing soil is not the same as bearing fruit. These practices do not bear fruit directly, but they prepare your life for it. Only the Spirit of God can produce spiritual fruit.

Because Jesus was divine, His emphasis in these practices was different than ours will be. (For example, Jesus didn't confess sin.) Different circumstances of life will also affect our practice of these things. For some, finding time and a place to work on them will be much more challenging than for others. For others, the demands of a young family, a heavy academic or work schedule may drive them to the brink of despair.

It can be a challenge to be personally committed to developing your spiritual life without its having unnecessary impact (sometimes perceived as negative impact) on those closest to you, especially family members. Simplicity may offer the biggest hurdle, followed by things like fasting, solitude, hospitality and service.

Let's consider the question posed in the initial text box of this section: Which is the better metaphor for the Christian life—marching or dancing? Our personal tendencies will incline us in one direction or the other. The Bible itself uses military imagery in relation to the Christian life, so there is a place for marching. Yet, when I read the accounts of God's interactions with His people, I don't see much of the straight line progress associated with soldiers moving in lock step across the parade square. (Soldiers haven't marched into battle for years.)

What Bible stories give us looks much more like dance—a step or two in one direction, a turn, a step or two in another direction, a turn, and so on. As He did with those who have gone before, I believe God longs for a relationship with us. He mostly desires us to move in step with Him, to find joy in the ever-shifting nuances of life as we live in growing intimacy with Him and the others who share it. I also believe that this calls for learning the steps, working on the patterns, watching and learning from others and mastering the art of following His lead.

The 19 ways to boost your spiritual life outlined here should help you not just become technically proficient as you move through life in relationship with God, they will also prepare you to enjoy that relationship in ways you may never have before.

Give yourself lots of time to work on these things. Some you'll struggle with, others will be almost as natural as breathing once you catch the idea. Some you'll have to work on one-by-one. Others will overlap nicely and give you a sense of where the whole process will end up.

As you work your way through these 19 ways to boost your spiritual life, remember to keep their purpose in mind. The objective is not to leave you feeling overwhelmed, but refreshed!

1. Find Quiet Space for Yourself

A story to start

Most of us spend a considerable amount of energy projecting ourselves to those around us. We have a fairly clear sense of how we want others to see us. But I think it would startle us if we knew how God perceives us. It shocked me. I am the son of the farmer, Joash. My name is Gideon.

During threshing time, you would typically find people on the hilltops. So I was quite sure that while hiding in the winepress, I would be safe from prying eyes. It was pathetically inefficient to thresh in the confines of the press, but at least, what grain I collected could be hidden and kept for my family. Those who thresh on the hilltops are almost inevitably robbed of their grain by the marauding Midianites.

I had told no one where I was, not even those closest to me. Each day before it got light, I would take as many sheaves as I could carry down to the winepress. For days I pursued my solitary occupation. It did not bother me to be alone. It gave me time to think, especially about the words of the prophet who had recently reminded the nation of our disobedience. As I rolled his words over in my mind, I got the strong impression that God was going to deliver us.

One day, as I beat the stalks of grain with my flail, I had the unnerving sensation of being watched. I chose this place because no one would normally come to the winepress at this time of year. The grapes were still green and hard. I had been careful to keep the whereabouts of my labour secret. Who could have followed me?

I looked around and at the foot of the ancient oak tree which shaded the press sat a man. Yet, was he a man? There was something unusual about him. He told me that, though I saw myself as the least significant member of the weakest clan in the altogether undistinguished tribe of Manasseh, God saw me as a mighty warrior. That was a shock. Who was this man to speak for God, especially a message which seemed patently absurd.

I prepared him a meal of meat and bread as I would for any stranger. When I presented it to him, he told me to put it on the rock. I complied and stepped back. Then, instead of eating it, he touched it with the tip of his staff. Instantly it burst into flames and disappeared. When I looked up, the stranger, too, was gone. This was no man, but an angel—the Angel of the Lord. That was how he found me, alone, in secret, in the least likely place for me to be.

So God has called me from the solitary task of threshing in secret to the solitary task of being His voice to His people for this time. He tells me I must drive out our enemies and guide the people back to Him. I have destroyed the altar of Baal. I have set the war trumpet to my lips and sent messengers through the land of the neighbouring tribes. Twice I have asked God to prove the legitimacy of the angel's message and it has been confirmed.

Tonight we camp beside the well of Harod, just across the valley from the Midianite encampment. May God rid us of this plague.

What are we talking about?

Finding quiet space for ourselves these days can be a challenge. Most of us live in situations where we have to share space. Often that shared space is full of distractions, but this only increases our need for solitude.

Solitude is being alone without being lonely.

Solitude is the positive counterpart to loneliness in which social isolation has negative consequences physically, emotionally and spiritually.

Solitude is typically chosen, while loneliness results from being alone against our will and wishes. For our purposes we will consider solitude to be a voluntary exercise which frees one from the obligations and influence of social interactions.

Biblical background

The following verses make it clear that Jesus both practised solitude Himself and encouraged His followers to do likewise. While very few Christians are called to the social isolation of the monastic life, as generally understood, we do need time away from other people to refresh and renew our spiritual vigour.

"*Now when Jesus heard this, he withdrew from there in a boat to a desolate place by himself. But when the crowds heard it, they followed him on foot from the towns*" (Matt. 14:13 ESV).

"*And after he had dismissed the crowds, he went up on the mountain by himself to pray. When evening came, he was there alone*" (Matt. 14:23 ESV).

"*And he said to them, 'Come away by yourselves to a desolate place and rest a while.' For many were coming and going, and they had no leisure even to eat*" (Mark 6:31 ESV).

Exploring solitude

Solitude tends to elicit a clear response from us, one way or the other. Some people crave time when they can be alone. Others do all they can to structure their time to avoid being alone. If they can't find someone to share their space, they turn on a radio or television to push back the sense of loneliness. While

Solitude helps us to...

...*follow Jesus' example*

...*free ourselves from the habit of letting others affect us*

...*free ourselves from the pathological need for other people*

...*embrace being alone without feeling lonely*

...*learn to be secure alone with God*

...*develop friendship with God*

...*learn what it means to "wait on the Lord"*

...*discover God's presence*

solitude requires us to be alone, I'm not talking about being lonely. Solitude is being alone without being lonely.

Solitude has several benefits, not the least of which is it sets us firmly in the path of Jesus. It frees us from the (often involuntary) tendency to be affected by others. Even when we try to not let this happen it does. Merely having someone else within earshot often inhibits us from praying aloud, for example. Solitude also frees us from the pathological aspects of our need for other people.

Some of us have never met ourselves. We have let other people define and identify us to such a degree that we don't know who we are unless someone else is nearby to tell us. Some people react negatively to solitude because they associate it with the pain of loneliness. In fact, solitude allows us to embrace being alone without feeling lonely. It teaches us to be secure when alone with God and to develop an intimate friendship with Him. Solitude will also provide opportunities to learn what it means to "wait on the Lord."

Waiting on the Lord includes two ideas associated with the word wait. We'll learn to wait in the sense of waiting for the bus—it's being in a state of readiness for His presence. We'll also learn to wait in the sense of waiting on tables—it's being engaged in service. It is good to be consciously serving God even when the physical manifestation of that service may be helping other people. Finally, most people find solitude an absolute necessity to discover the reality of God's presence.

There is a wonderful role for fellowship in our lives, but there is also a place for quiet intimacy with God which is not shared with anyone else.

Once you've successfully spent a few hours entirely alone with God, follow the instructions on the shampoo bottle—repeat.

Here are a few practical suggestions to get you started in your practice of solitude. Like all of the *19 ways to boost your spiritual life*, you'll have to be intentional about this. Opportunities rarely present themselves unbidden.

Find Quiet Space for Yourself

Find a place where you can be alone. Not only should it be a place without people, but it should also be free of potential interruptions, so no communication devices. To start, schedule a time to go to that place. I'm not asking you to be legalistic, but if you're anything like me, you'll have to be firm with yourself. Our culture is geared to busyness. We accept it. We expect it. We respect it. You'll be bucking the trend to do this.

> *Whether media reflects or sets the agenda for culture, ask yourself about the last time you saw a lead character who wasn't desperately overworked or trying to get a relationship going. "Busy" sells because it's what the majority relates to best.*

As you develop your taste for solitude try taking a three or four day retreat by yourself. There are retreat centres that offer opportunities for this. Other options include tenting in a provincial park, or in the back field of a farmer friend. If the idea of being that close to nature doesn't appeal to you and you have the resources, book an overnight in an economical hotel. For some, work or family obligations may make it impossible to get away for any significant period. Be creative. Start with a few hours alone in a park or library. These options cost nothing and provide a quiet setting which will suit your purposes.

Between your planned times of solitude take control of intrusive media devices by turning them off for specific periods as you are able. While some professions require people to be "on-call," much of our tendency to be available 24/7 is generated by our own sense of indispensability.

One last suggestion, intentionally look for intervals during the day when you can have some private, quiet time to regroup and refocus on the spiritual significance of your life. If you struggle to find anything of spiritual significance, consider that your response to various circumstances may have caused you to shut down emotionally. This is bound to have a negative impact on our spiritual lives. While the emotional and spiritual realms do not overlap completely, emotional coldness with others, even with just a single individual, can have a chilling effect on our relationship with God.

John made this clear when he wrote: *"If anyone says, 'I love God,' and hates his brother, he is a liar; for he who does not love his brother whom he has seen cannot love God whom he has not seen"* (1 John 4:20 ESV). What is true in an absolute sense here is also true in relative terms. To the degree that I am estranged from those God calls me to love, I am estranged from God.

A few signs that you're not getting enough solitude

Some time ago, the website of the Swedish Medical Center offered this list of ten symptoms that indicate the need for some solitude.

- Irritability
- Anger at those closest to you
- A feeling of being overly-intruded upon
- Not wanting to do things you normally want to do
- Fatigue
- Nervousness
- Confusion
- Shakiness
- Lack of energy
- Tight breathing

Some of these symptoms, especially in combination, could easily be confused with a panic attack—perhaps even constitute a panic attack.

I can't think of any better advice to deal with this list of symptoms than the words of Jesus I quoted earlier. You'll recall that the disciples were coming and going at such a hectic pace they had no leisure time at all, not even enough to sit back and enjoy a meal. In this pressure-cooker ministry environment, Jesus told them *"Come away by yourselves to a desolate place and rest a while"* (Mark 6:31 ESV). It doesn't get better than that. Not for the original twelve disciples. Not for us.

Potential pitfalls

Anything as good as solitude must, at the same time, have dangers to be avoided. In its more extreme forms solitude can lead to withdrawal from engaging with and serving others. If you have a strong inclination to introversion, you might need to be careful to avoid using solitude to legitimize escape. Regardless of our personality type, solitude could prompt us to become unduly focussed on ourselves.

A word of encouragement

One of the good old things about the good old days, that younger generations get tired of hearing about, was that our forefathers were closer to their agrarian roots than most of us are. This often forced people to live somewhat isolated lives, especially in winter. A certain level of solitude was unavoidable and considered normal. Not so now. Most of us will have to make a deliberate attempt to practise solitude at even an elementary level. It's tough, but it can be done. Not only can it be done, but it can also be a significant help in moving you into a deeper relationship with God.

2. Be Quiet

A story to start

Fear, despair, self-pity, depression—not usually the hallmarks of a person who walks with God—but, I know them well. I have walked uninvited into the presence of royalty. I have spoken directly to a king. I have turned my back and walked away with my head held high. I have run for my life until I was exhausted and wanted to die. I am Elijah the Tishbite.

The knock on my door had an authoritative ring to it. The man outside, in uniform, bore a message from Queen Jezebel. She had signed my death warrant. My execution was to take place within 24 hours. He left abruptly. So did I.

I made it out of Israel, into Judah and headed south into the wilderness. While my feet ran, so did my mind. I rehearsed the events of the last few years. In my agitation, the mental pictures of recent days continually interrupted. I kept seeing the anger in the king's eyes, the contempt on his wife's face, the strength of the messenger's jaw as he announced my death sentence.

Over and over, the pictures flashed in my mind. I was only vaguely aware of the desert through which I ran. I didn't even stop to drink. In my haste to get away, I had brought no provisions. I was growing weaker. Reason teetered on the brink. I was the only man of God left. When the Queen tracked me down and killed me, the voice of God would be silenced. But there was no silence for me. Jumbled thoughts collided in my mind while distracting voices brought me ever nearer to despair. When I could go no further, I fell in a heap under a juniper tree. Rehearsing my sad situation one last time, I begged God to take my life.

Twice I was awakened and given food by an angel. I thought it was a dream, but it must have been real for I gained great strength from it—enough strength to make it all the way to Horeb, the mountain of God. There I crawled into a cave and again collapsed.

Here, far from Ahab and the murderous Jezebel, in this quiet place, my mind began to settle. In the quietness there, little by little, I was able to quieten the clamouring voices in my mind. Peace at last. No one to talk to. No one to listen to. No sounds at all in my subterranean refuge.

As I lay there for a long time in total quietness I gradually became aware of a stirring in my spirit. The word of the Lord challenged me. I was ready for this and responded with my prepared answer. I said it out loud and the words echoing in the cave sounded exceedingly grand. "I have been very jealous for the LORD, the God of hosts. For the people of Israel have forsaken your covenant, thrown down your altars, and killed your prophets with the sword, and I, even I only, am left, and they seek my life, to take it away."[1] There was a long pause. It was gratifying to have silenced God. Then came the impression, "Go out and stand on the mountain."

I made my way out of the darkness into the sunshine at the mouth of the cave. Suddenly a mighty storm blew in. God Himself was walking on the mountains. Great boulders were torn from the mountainside and hurtled past me. I stood protected in the mouth of the cave, but trembled at the power that was being displayed a little more than an arm's length in front of me.

Then I dropped to my knees. The wind had stopped, but the earth was shaking—violently. I couldn't even kneel. I lay on the ground. The ground at the mouth of the cave seemed as agitated as my soul.

When the earthquake subsided, the whole mountain outside erupted into flame. I lifted my head to watch the spectacle. I pulled my cloak across my face to protect myself from the scorching heat. What was God doing in these displays of power? What was He saying to me?

Then, as suddenly as it began, the fire ended. I expected the whole mountainside to be consumed, but the grasses and wild flowers were unscorched. The trees were still green. It was quiet. Profound silence filled the place. It was even quieter here than it had been in the cave. Out of this empty space came a voice. It was not simply an inner impression of the Lord speaking to me as He had so many times in the past. This was the voice of God in sound waves, vibrating my ear drums. God speaking to me.

What are we talking about?

Being quiet calls us to find a place of relative silence. Silence is simply the absence of sound or noise. "Sound" is meaningful in that it carries information. Speech and music serve as good examples. However, even sounds can lose their significance if we don't understand or refuse to process the signals. "Noise" is meaningless in that it carries no information. Examples of this include traffic noise and refrigerator hum. However, these noises can convey information about the functioning of their source. For our purposes, we are principally concerned with inner quiet – the shutting out of any and all distracting messages so that we can hear from God. At first it is easier to achieve this inner stillness in quiet environments. As you practise, you will be able to find it even amid the noise and sounds of everyday life.

"it is in deep solitude that I find the gentleness with which I can truly love my brothers. The more solitary I am the more affection I have for them.... Solitude and silence teach me to love my brothers for what they are, not for what they say."[2]

Biblical background

Inner quietness (supported by external silence) has long been a part of the spiritual development of God's people. To underscore this fact, let's look at four Old Testament references:

"When He gives quietness, who then can make trouble? And when He hides His face, who then can see Him, whether it is against a nation or a man alone?" (Job 34:29 NKJV).

"*Better is a dry morsel with quietness, than a house full of feasting with strife.*" (Prov. 17:1 NKJV).

"*Better a handful with quietness than both hands full, together with toil and grasping for the wind*" (Eccl. 4:6 NKJV).

"*For thus says the Lord God, the Holy One of Israel: 'In returning and rest you shall be saved; in quietness and confidence shall be your strength.' But you would not...* " (Isa. 30:15 NKJV).

In his letter, James encourages us to be *"swift to hear, slow to speak, slow to wrath"* (Jas. 1:19 NKJV). This advice highlights a tendency that most of us have. We are quicker to speak than to listen. If we include our own voices among the sources of sound and noise that we "turn off," we will learn the benefit of James' admonition. Doing so will help us to hear what others are trying to tell us, but, more importantly, we'll be able to hear God.

Exploring quietness

"Noise tends to increase stress levels which in turn can result in increased frustration, anger and strained interpersonal relationships. We must begin to establish a friendship with silence."[3]

At first when you seek to be quiet, you'll discover that there is a lot of noise in the environment which you unconsciously filter. Everyone who attempts to find quietness has to deal with this. It's principally a matter of identifying and tuning out the sounds that surround you. Little can be done about them and it's amazing how little they bother you once you've recognized them and chosen to ignore them. But you'll barely be finished with this exercise and you'll discover another intrusion—what I call "mental racket" inside your own head. In the quiet, you'll learn to identify and still your inner voices—the thoughts that intrude the moment you stop concentrating on something else.

Most of us share the compulsion to talk. When we are with others, we are subject to their desire to express themselves. At

Be Quiet

times this can be truly helpful, encouraging, uplifting. But at other times, what others say is distracting, discouraging and at times even destructive. Being quiet will necessitate our getting away from others occasionally in order to mute the noise both within and without. Already you can see that these *19 ways to boost your spiritual life* cannot be effectively practised in isolation. They go together, each built on, and providing a foundation for, others.

One of the great surrogates of conversation these days is the communications media. For some, it is tough to get control over these sound sources. Much of the media conveys a spiritually negative message. They are designed to attract an audience by giving the audience what it wants and what it wants is a message that reinforces its natural inclinations toward sinful experience and self-expression.

Quietness frees us from the demands of the world. The incessant cries of advertisers attempting to create dissatisfaction in our souls almost forces us to cave in. The broadcast voices

Join me in one of my own exercises. I'm writing this very early on a winter morning. It is still outside so everything I hear is generated inside the house. The first thing I notice and choose to ignore is the ringing in my ears (I have tinnitus). Other sounds in my environment include:

*-the warm air being pushed into the room by the furnace fan
-the computer fan on my laptop
-the rubbing of my mouse on the desk as I scroll back to check something
-the ping of my mug hitting the plate as I set it down and percussive thud of contact
-the sound of chewing and swallowing my morning toast
-the sound of my heart beating
-the clicking of the computer keys
-the mew of a hungry cat in the next room*

It's amazing—the sounds lurking about awaiting detection!

of the current generation of experts tell us how to develop a healthy menu, raise successful children, maximize our potential and more. These can lay a tremendous sense of obligation on us if we don't take occasional breaks and renew our spiritual perspective.

> **Silence helps us to...**
> ...learn to listen (especially to God)
> ...learn to identify (and silence) our inner voices
> ...free ourselves from the distraction of other voices (media as well as individuals)
> ...free ourselves from the demands of the world
> ...learn to surrender control—no input, no influence
> ...experience God's peace

I recently heard about a woman who had a popcorn kernel caught in her larynx, rendering her literally speechless for almost four months. When she finally was able to speak again, she told people that during that time she had learned to listen as she never had before. Often when others are talking, much of our mental energy goes into formulating what we want to say in response. When the ability to make a quick reply was taken away, she could focus on the incoming message. At the same time, of course, this reduced her influence. After all, if we have no input, we have no influence. In a conversation, we need to be able to speak in order to steer the discussion. When we keep quiet, we learn to surrender control. This can be very positive because it forces us to set aside our own selfish agenda for the sake of others and prepares us to listen to God.

Potential pitfalls

It is hard to imagine any particular danger that might be associated with being quiet, other than perhaps addiction! Many things in which we engage for our spiritual benefit can be abused in one way or another. However, as long as you are maintaining healthy relationships with the people in your life, you are unlikely to suffer any negative consequences from adding some quiet times to your daily routine.

A word of encouragement

Before leaving the quiet place, I'll mention that it is often in silence that we experience God's peace. As long as we are expressing our dissatisfaction, our pain, our discontent, our grief, even in prayer, we drown out the incoming message of God for us. Finding a quiet place and then silencing our own inner voices allows us to experience the comfort and peace of God we would otherwise miss. Psalm 46 is famous for telling us: *"Be still and know that I am God"* (Psalm 46:10 NKJV). One of the ways to translate "still" in this verse is with the word "quiet." In other words, "Be quiet and know that I am God.

"True silence is the rest of the mind; it is to the spirit what sleep is the body: nourishment and refreshment."[3]

---

1. 1 Kings 19:10 ESV
2. Merton, Thomas—www.quotationspage.com/subjects/ silence/31.html
3. Moore, Mike—www.naturalhealthweb.com/articles/moore4.html
4. Penn, William—www.quotationspage.com/subjects/ silence/31.html

3. Confess Your Faults

A story to start

Some of us are burdened with a complex identity which makes it hard for us to know ourselves. I ask myself, "Am I a warrior, a poet, a man after God's own heart, a sin-riddled rebel, a king over people, or a slave to my passions?" I am all of these. I am David, king of Israel, admired for my strengths, reviled for my weakness, but loved of God.

Yesterday, I wrote a poem. I've written many. It's what I do when my soul is troubled. Publicly I go through the motions of being the king. I make decisions, render judgments, engage in diplomacy and plan conquests, but remorse gnaws my inward parts. I have been a fool, a coward, a traitor to one who loved and served me well.

The hand of God has been heavy upon me of late. Part of me would like to go to the temple. Perhaps the blood-letting there would wash away my guilt. But the sight of the innocent animal thrashing in its death-throes fades before my eyes as I imagine noble Uriah slashed by an Ammonite sword. People praise my imagination when they read my poetry, but to me it is a curse as I see things in my mind as clearly as if they were happening before me. God cleanse my mind! Wipe away these pictures!

I would go to the temple and endure the bloody horrors there, but it would do no good. God does not take delight in sacrifices of this kind. What He wants is the sacrifice of my own heart—not torn from my body as I deserve, but beating strongly with deepest passion for Him.

O God, deliver me from the guilt of my shameful selfishness—my worthy servant's heart pierced physically, his gentle wife's tortured emotionally. I struggle to look at her in these days when my own heart is the home of a thousand daggers, each one double-edged and twisted by the hand of a skilled swordsman.

Pictures plague me. Some of my own making, others insuppressible memories. Why can I not forget the old prophet's bony finger, pointing at me, his king. No one would dare point a finger at a king. Send him to the executioner for such disrespect! But this is not merely Nathan's finger. It is the finger of God and I cannot bear it. It stabs the air, but my heart is pierced.

O God, I confess my sin again to you. I have confessed to Nathan to whom you revealed everything. I have poured out my contrition to Bathsheba. In my dreams I have wept at the grave of Uriah. These things can never happen again. Only when my heart is truly washed clean and set fully on You can You take any pleasure in my spiritual exercise.

O God, wash me whiter than snow. Bring the sounds of joy and gladness back to my life. Blot out my sin so that my failings and your forgiveness can stand forever as a record of your love for the children of men.

What are we talking about?

Confession is the acknowledgment, disclosure or admission of sin. Three aspects of confession capture our attention:

- Confession to God to access His forgiveness.
- Confession to someone whom we have wronged as we ask for forgiveness.
- Confession to another person of a personal weakness or besetting sin to solicit prayer, spiritual support and accountability.

We will touch on all three areas to some extent. I assume most of us have personal knowledge of the first two, but confession of our struggle with recurring sin is the area of confession with which many of us are quite unfamiliar because it is not a regular part of many traditions. Yet, I believe it is significant because repeated failing tends to make us give up, consigning ourselves to spiritual mediocrity at best and often outright defeat.

A personal reflection

As a child, I grew up in an Irish Catholic farming community. My identity was shaped, in part, by the fact that I lived only on the fringe of that community. When I walked with the neighbour children to catch the school bus, we were just a bunch of farm kids. We shared that aspect of life. But when we got off the bus, some differences surfaced. They went to one school, I went to another. They went to mass every day, I didn't. They didn't eat meat on Fridays, I did. They went to confession on Saturday evenings, I didn't. I believe that my own negative perception of confession began there. It was a short jump from knowing I didn't have to confess my sins to any human mediator for forgiveness to thinking that I should never confess my sins to another person.

The Biblical Background

The most direct Bible passage dealing with confessing our sins to each other is the one where James directs his readers to *"Confess your trespasses to one another, and pray for one another, that you may be healed. The effective, fervent prayer of a righteous man avails much"* (Jas. 5:16 NKJV). The context suggests that sin can lead to physical ailments and that confession of that sin and prayer support can bring healing and freedom.

Paul comes at the issue from the other side in his letter to the Galatians. He wrote, *"If anyone is caught in any transgression, you who are spiritual should restore him in a spirit of gentleness. Keep watch on yourself, lest you too be tempted. Bear one another's burdens, and so fulfill the law of Christ"* (Gal. 6:1-2 ESV). Here Paul shows that Christians have the responsibility of restoring and supporting those whose sin has come into the open.

> Confession is uncomfortable because it makes us vulnerable. It lets others see into our souls.
>
> Most of us would like to keep the dark part of ourselves in the dark.

Exploring confession

Bringing your own sin into the open is never comfortable, but several passages note its importance. Solomon recorded: *"Whoever conceals his transgressions will not prosper, but he who confesses and forsakes them will obtain mercy"* (Pro. 28:13 ESV). Note in particular that confession and repentance go together. When we confess and abandon our sin we will find mercy. However, when we hide our sin, we are seldom motivated to repent of it. It seems to take some level of public knowledge to motivate us to repent. That "public knowledge" may be as minimal as one other person knowing, but I know from experience that even one other person's knowing of my weakness motivates me to forsake it.

This would probably be a good place to emphasize that when I talk about confession here, I am not talking about confession to God for pardon. I have in mind confessing our sin to another person. I believe that person should be a wise, discrete, mature Christian. Much harm can be done by being too public about private matters, yet we can easily remain trapped in sin if we don't get it out there at least in some limited way.

There are many good reasons to practise confession. It will help us develop personal humility. Few things humble our pride like confessing our sin to someone else. It reminds us of the grim fact that we are sinners and depend entirely on God's grace to have any hope at all for the future.

Confession helps us to...
...develop personal humility
...develop transparency
...practise authentic living
...encourage others to live honestly
...promote genuine fellowship (we relate to real people rather than psychological projections)
...experience spiritual freedom (secret sins are very strong and destructive)
...experience the love of God inspite of our sin

Confession also helps us to develop transparency. It is wonderfully freeing to know that no hidden sin lurks in the shadows to bring you shame. If someone thinks they have uncovered some secret sin in your life, it is comforting to have another person who can step forward and say, "I knew about that and we're working together on defeating it."

Personal transparency not only allows us to live authentically, it also encourages others to live authentically. When Christians pretend to be perfect, it makes the rest of us flawed souls think that we are great failures who must hide our sin to be accepted. When others know of our weaknesses, they are free to seek help for theirs.

> "It is not the criminal things that are hardest to confess, but the ridiculous and the shameful."[1]

Understand that nothing can be hidden from God and most things cannot be hidden from those closest to us. Search your heart and discover the sin there, so you can confess it. Invite someone close to you to point out the weaknesses to which you are blind, so you can deal with them as well. Ask God to shine His light into your life to identify anything that offends Him, so you can clear those things out of the way. Once you have been cleansed and forgiven, commit to living that way.

Confess your sin as soon as you become aware of it. Commit to calling sin what it is—we have so many polite words for specific sins. We "mislead" or "deceive" instead of lying. We "borrow" instead of stealing. We "have an affair" instead of committing adultery. Use the ugly words for sins. It'll help you remember to avoid them. Give up pretending that sin is an option

> "In confession... we open our lives to healing, reconciling, restoring, uplifting grace of Him who loves us in spite of what we are."[2]

for you. Understand that confession, for the Christian, is not limited to asking for forgiveness for sins past, but includes resolve to avoid sins future. Finally, accept the seriousness of confession—false or superficial confession without repentance is pointless.

Potential pitfalls

Some dangers are associated with confession. Some of us can engage in confession to draw attention to ourselves. We shouldn't confess to impress. We confess to experience forgiveness and enlist support. Some use confession to legitimize self-obsession. We shouldn't confess to obsess. We confess to experience freedom. Some of us find confession a handy tool for deflecting blame with words like "I've done it again. He (or she) did that thing (or said those words) and I just reacted." We shouldn't confess to assess blame. We confess to take ownership of our sin and deal with it.

A word of encouragement

Here's one way confession might look in the context of a married couple: "Jules and Olivia are in their fifties, and even though their children are grown, they love to celebrate Shabbos. Every Friday night before the Sabbath meal, they draw a warm bath and, together, take off their clothes and bathe. This is their ritual cleansing, part of their marriage covenant, preparation to receive the Sabbath bride. But more than this, it is also a time for intimacies, and confession.

"Each unclothed and open to receive the other, they each put a hand to the other's heart, and ask if there is anything they need to say, any confession, something lingering in the heart that, left unsaid, would hinder a full and joyful Sabbath. On some nights, there is little to say. On other nights, words must be spoken aloud that have lived in secret. Who can imagine what lovers must share, when seeking a pure heart and an honest Sabbath? For thirty years, such honesty comes to this: two beings, warm and close, bathed in love."[3]

---

1. Rousseau, Jean Jacques (1712-1778) — www.realtime.net/~wdoud/topics/confession.html
2. Cassels, Louis — www.realtime.net/~wdoud/topics/confession.html
3. Muller, Wayne in "Sabbath: Finding Rest, Renewal, and Delight in our Busy Lives" N.Y., Bantam Books, 1999, p.198

4. Meditate

A story to start

To be young and in ministry is a challenge at any time. But to be young, in ministry, far from home and by yourself can seem overwhelming. I understand this because it is the situation in which I find myself. I am Paul's protégé, Timothy.

I sometimes look out of my window over the teeming city and wonder how a small-town boy from Lystra ended up in the biggest city in Asia Minor. Some are saying Ephesus is second only to Rome in size and influence. And here I am trying to be an influence for righteousness in the city that is most famous for the fanatical worship of Artemis, or Diana, as the Romans call her.

It has been a challenge from the start. Most of the believers are older than I am and I wonder whether they think I'm up for the job. My years of travelling with Paul and the rest of the missionary team gives me some credibility, but I'm not finding my youth a great asset.

I'm grateful that though Paul is still travelling, he remembers to send letters back to me and to the church here. He knows me so well, he can anticipate the struggles I'm having. More than that, he offers good advice. He reminds me to not let my youthful appearance be a disadvantage to me. I sometimes worry about that.

Actually, I'm learning to replace worry with meditation. Paul suggested this. He gave me several things to meditate on. He emphasized reading the Scriptures, my ministry of encouragement, the teaching of the apostles and my own spiritual gift.

At first I found it hard to focus on these things, as my mind would keep drifting back to the problems I'm facing. Frankly, I'm a bit homesick—to the point of having stomach problems, and the competing approaches to spiritual life here are wearing me down. Sometimes preachers want to present messages that sound more like law than grace.

So meditation has been a lifeline for me. As I spend time thinking about the positive things Paul suggested, God's Spirit revives me. I'm reminded of the old days when we travelled together, Paul, Silas, Luke and the others. I'm so glad they let me tag along. To be that close to these men of God and listen to what God was showing them as they meditated on His word, was the best education a young man could hope for.

Now, I'm on my own here and others are looking to me. Paul reminds me to be a good example. I guess if I use him as my example, I won't lead others astray. And slowly, the Scriptures are giving me confidence. Paul has written some letters to the churches which the other apostles are placing on the same level as the Torah. That is exciting.

Some people think Paul is somewhat arrogant and proud, but I know the man. He's even included my name as co-author of some of the letters written when we were travelling together. They were special times and I like to meditate on them when I'm starting to feel a little overwhelmed.

What are we talking about?

Let me establish immediately that in encouraging Christians to meditate, I am not suggesting a Christianized variation of any of the Eastern forms of meditation. Biblical meditation is entirely different. It is unfortunate that there is confusion over the word and the way different faiths use it. I considered alternatives and nothing as good as the biblical word carried the concept so well. So, with this in mind, let's think about what biblical meditation is, how to practise it, and some of the benefits that can come of it.

I don't know who first said "If you know how to worry, you already know how to meditate." But I know that it's been repeated thousands of times – just check it on your favourite search engine. Though not very profound, this expression is helpful in explaining meditation to people who have no experience with it. Like worry, meditation involves rehearsing something over in your mind, looking at it from different angles and trying to understand all of the possible outcomes and their ramifications. The difference is worry is negative and rooted in our physical circumstances while meditation is positive and focusses on our spiritual reality.

Biblical background

Meditation is as old as the Bible. God charged Joshua with these words at the beginning of his time of leadership: *"This Book of the Law shall not depart from your mouth, but you shall meditate on it day and night, so that you may be careful to do according to all that is written in it. For then you will make your way prosperous, and then you will have good success"* (Josh. 1:8 ESV).

The Psalms contain many references to meditation. Paying particular attention to the subjects of the Psalmists' meditation, consider these representative ones:

"My soul will be satisfied as with fat and rich food, and my mouth will praise you with joyful lips, when I remember you upon my bed, and meditate on you in the watches of the night" (Psalms 63:5-6 ESV).

"But his [the one who is blessed] *delight is in the law of the LORD, and on his law he meditates day and night"* (Psalms 1:2 ESV).

"My eyes are awake before the watches of the night, that I may meditate on your promise" (Psalms 119:148 ESV).

"I remember the days of old; I meditate on all that you have done; I ponder the work of your hands" (Psalms 143:5 ESV)

In the New Testament, Paul wrote to Timothy: *"Meditate on these things* [Paul's encouragement, the Scriptures, Timothy's spiritual gifts]*; give yourself entirely to them, that your progress may be evident to all"* (1 Tim. 4:15 NKJV).

Exploring meditation

Meditation got a bad name among Christians in the 1960's when Eastern Mysticism penetrated North American culture in various forms—some religiously based, others supposedly not. This was an unfortunate turn of events because serious Christians have been meditating for centuries to deepen their spiritual life. To separate what I am talking about here from other kinds of meditation I will tell you that what I have in mind is intentional, conscious, spiritual rumination of a scriptural detail.

Meditation has value for several reasons. It allows us to deepen our understanding of God as we carefully consider who He is and what He has done for us. As this happens, it is inevitable that our appreciation for God will deepen as well. Together, a growing understanding of and appreciation for God refreshes, comforts and encourages our spirit. Living in a world where there is so much anti-God expression, we can benefit greatly from this. It concerns many in Christian leadership that believers seem to slide quite easily into a secular world view between Sundays.

Meditation helps us to...
...deepen our understanding of and appreciation for God
...refresh, comfort and encourage our own spirit
...make beneficial use of otherwise wasted moments

If you take a moment to flip back to the Psalms mentioned in the "Biblical background" section, you'll notice several subjects for the believer's meditation. God, Himself, tops the list. If you need some help to get started, think about those "compare and contrast" assignments of high-school English classes. Consider how God is like and unlike other persons and things that you know and relate to in everyday life. He will inevitably surpass them all and in the process of this meditation, you will align your thinking with reality.

A second worthy subject, also brought to us in the Psalms is "the law of the Lord," and by extension, we could include all of Scripture. Here is an exhaustless supply of uplifting themes. Take a verse, a phrase, even just a word (one of the great ones like, "justified" or "redeemed" or "fellowship") and come at it from every perspective you can think of. These would include, but not be limited to, your own, God's (all three persons), your fellow-believers (be they here, or in the persecuted church), unbelievers, angels, demons, and so on. Wrestle with the idea within your own mind.

The promises of God comprise another field bearing a rich harvest for the meditating mind. Just think of all that God offers us, blessings in this world and the next. Don't let me get started listing them! Besides, there are whole books written to draw them to your attention if you need help.

One final suggestion is to meditate on "the work of God's hands." This may be best done lying on your back staring into a starry sky or gazing through sun-dappled leaves in the forest. Wherever you do it, though, revel in the marvels of God's creation which cannot be catalogued.

Paul expands the list of worthy themes for meditation in his epistle of joy. *"Finally, brothers, whatever is true, whatever is honourable, whatever is just, whatever is pure, whatever is lovely, whatever is commendable, if there is any excellence, if there is anything worthy of praise, think about these things"* (Phil. 4:8 ESV).

Potential pitfalls

There is only one negative item to consider here and that is the possibility that the meditation I've been describing might be confused with psychological/spiritual techniques used to induce an altered state of consciousness. Our purpose is not to lose touch with reality, but to connect with reality.

Besides simply being aware of the potential confusion, we can further minimize any hazard of ending up where we don't want to go by staying focussed. As I can attest from personal experience, unfocussed stillness often leads to sleep. So it is important to occupy your mind, not empty it (as is often encouraged in other forms of meditation). You might memorize a sentence or two from Scripture and ruminate on them or choose an aspect of God's character and think about its significance. If you choose an exalted theme to meditate on, the results can't help being positive.

One useful safeguard is to begin any time of meditation by purposefully asking God to lead your thoughts by His Holy Spirit. This will not only keep your mind from running down unprofitable pathways, but will open it to receive the light that He will bring to bear on the passage or subject on which you are meditating.

A word of encouragement

Don't be deterred by those who would, in their knee-jerk desire to eliminate all risk, discourage you from this thoroughly biblical activity. By all means be wise, but don't be afraid to pursue God with all of the resources He has given you. Learn what it is to love him with your mind as the first and greatest commandment requires.

5. Serve Others

A story to start

What could bring greater joy to a servant than to be offered more demanding work? I am about to head off on the greatest adventure of my life so far. Such a responsibility. Such an honour. I am Phoebe, servant of the church in Cenchrea.

Two weeks ago, Paul passed through here on his way from Corinth to Jerusalem. He and his companions were carrying the relief money from our part of the world to help our brothers and sisters in Jerusalem. Paul and his companions were nervous. The whole bunch of them. I thought it was about the money, but that was only part of it.

During their time in Corinth, Paul and Tertius had been writing a letter to the church in Rome. I can just imagine poor old Tertius trying to keep up with the torrent of Paul's words. His thoughts often seem complex the first time you hear them. Not only did Tertius have to hear and understand them, but he had to write them down. And he had to do it quickly. At any rate, they finished just as they were ready to head to Jerusalem. For security reasons, they wanted to stay together and needed someone to carry the letter to Rome.

On the Lord's day, after we had met for teaching and worship, Paul asked me for a few minutes to talk something over. He thanked me for the work I've done for the church here in Cenchrea. Ever since my husband died, I've had quite a bit of time on my hands and I could think of nothing better to do than to spend it with some of the other widows and a few infirm folk who are part of our fellowship.

No one else seems to have much time for them and they do struggle to get out to do even the simplest chores. I find myself running errands, carrying messages, going to the market and other things they find overwhelming. Having just had my 51st birthday, I still have lots of energy and some of the other dear widows are well on in years. Along with the physical help I try to be to them, I have been making it a point to encourage them spiritually as well.

Because of this, my service was recently recognized by the elders here and now I am known as "a servant of the church." I feel entirely unworthy, but the brothers here felt it was important for me to be known this way because I've also been given responsibility to distribute some financial help to my less fortunate friends. This is a huge benefit to them and a great joy to me.

There, I've gone and distracted myself. I was telling you about Paul thanking me for my deacon work here. Then he totally surprised me by telling me that he had spoken to the elders and together they had decided that I should have a short break from my usual activities.

Paul proposed that I carry his letter to Rome and deliver it to the church there. This is a very valuable document. It has some of the most important doctrines God has ever given Paul. As they considered who should have this responsibility, they thought of me. Paul said it was for two reasons: I had proven myself faithful and because no one, especially the enemies of the gospel, would ever guess that I, a widow, would be entrusted with such an important task.

So here I am, finishing up my preparations. My daughter-in-law has only one child and she's volunteered to visit my little circle of friends who need help and encouragement. My daughter is coming with me, mostly for the sake of appearances. If I travelled alone, I would be noticed. But a widow and her daughter going to Rome to visit her husband's family? Entirely unremarkable!

Paul has been so grateful and kind. He and Tertius added some personal greetings to the letter and provided a little introduction for me, asking the Christians in Rome to be as helpful to me as they can. I'm excited about this trip. I've only been to Rome once before and that was a long time ago. Pray for me when you think of me. I feel the responsibility before me very deeply.

Serve Others

What are we talking about?

Service is that activity which is helpful to, or benefits, someone else, typically at some cost to one's self, in the expenditure of energy if not other resources as well. It is worth noting that the Greek word which is most often translated "servant" is "doulos." This word is best translated as "slave." I once heard John MacArthur point out in a radio program that it is only the squeamishness of the translators that prompts them to soften that word to "servant" in most English translations.

Biblical background

For our purposes, we'll chiefly consider these words of Jesus: *"You know that the rulers of the Gentiles lord it over them, and their great ones exercise authority over them. It shall not be so among you. But whoever would be great among you must be your servant, and whoever would be first among you must be your slave, even as the Son of Man came not to be served but to serve, and to give his life as a ransom for many"* (Matt. 20:25-28 ESV).

I have been reading leadership literature in a serious way since about 1990. Many times, in both secular and Christian books and articles, this saying of Jesus (or at least part of it) is quoted for the benefit of contemporary leaders. When we serve, we put the specific needs of others first while meeting a common goal. The "others" may be either individuals or a group of some kind, in our context, usually the church. Service reminds us that we are not the reason for our work. We are focussed on something bigger than ourselves. We serve to fulfill that higher purpose, either

"When Jesus took a towel to wash His disciples' feet, He completely redefined what leadership and service are. He made the point that they are not about pride or position in the world, but rather our position in Him."[1]

directly, or indirectly by facilitating the service of others so that they can make the greatest contribution possible. Service may be humble, but it is noble.

Exploring service

There are at least a couple of distortions related to service in the Christian life. I realize I have a hard sell before me with this topic. Those who tend to be consumers will be quick to remind us that everything we have is of grace—works do not benefit us. Those who tend to be servers are typically already stretched to the breaking point and the last thing they want to hear is someone encouraging them to find new ways to serve.

It is true that works of service do not benefit us. They benefit others. That's what they are for. It's also true that people with a servant's heart tend to overcommit. They need encouragement to refine their service according to their spiritual gifts and to stop trying to do everything.

Jesus' teaching on service stands our usual attitude toward greatness and leadership on its head, pointing out that the truly great people of our world are those who serve others. The real power of Jesus' words are not in the words themselves, but in the way He lived them out—giving His life as a ransom for many. Clearly, true followers of Jesus, those who really want to be like Him, must approach life with the same attitude toward others. Serving intentionally will certainly make us more like Jesus.

"The Discipline of Service is not to please people, but to please God with all our heart! It is not about getting public opinion or people on our side; it is leaning on God's side."[2]

Service also gives us opportunities to learn about humility. There is a strange kind of false humility abroad in Christian circles which exalts the workaholic believer. But genuine service, done entirely for the benefit of the other, is associated with true humility. It is hard to know which comes first. Do we serve because we are humble, or are we humble because we serve? Either way, the two go together. Choosing to serve reorients us from self-centred to others-centred living.

> "For even the Son of Man did not come to be served, but to serve, and to give His life a ransom for many" (Mark 10:45 ESV).

Service also teaches us that our significance is not in becoming grander, but in raising others up. True greatness comes from building into the lives of others, not building monuments to ourselves. Some only want to serve in what they consider to be significant roles, shunning the menial and seemingly meaningless opportunities that come along. In fact, all service is equal. It is the servant's heart that pleases God, not just the specific acts of service we perform. We often focus on the works themselves, ignoring the spirit in which we might do them.

Service is valuable to us in a broader sense because it gives us opportunities to learn to let others be in control. Most of us hate the sensation of being "out of control." This is only a problem when we delude ourselves in one of two ways. In the normal course of events in relationships, either we are in control so everything seems right to us, or the other is in control leading us to expect disaster at every turn. The fact is that God is in control, whether He is working through us or someone else. So on one level, surrendering control makes us feel vulnerable because we fear others may take advantage of us. On a higher level, surrendering control to God teaches us to

> "Everybody can be great... because anybody can serve. You don't have to have a college degree to serve. You don't have to make your subject and verb agree to serve. You only need a heart full of grace. A soul generated by love."[3]

rest in Him and puts us in the position where we can benefit from whatever circumstances in which we find ourselves.

Potential pitfalls

As with all of these *19 ways to boost our spiritual life*, there is a potential pitfall in service. The danger is that we may engage in service to others to meet our own needs. This, of course, is a perversion of the very concept of service, yet it is a common problem. True service is performed for the benefit of others, not for ourselves. We may receive some personal pleasure from it. We may receive gratitude from the ones we serve. We may even get some recognition in the broader community. But we must guard against the tendency to be motivated by the pleasure, the gratitude and the recognition. A good question to ask yourself in this regard is "Am I engaging in this act of service to please God, those I serve, or myself?"

A word of encouragement

Where possible, practise secrecy in your service. Be neither ostentatious nor deceptive. Don't use your ability and willingness to serve as a badge of honour. Train yourself to look for situations where you can serve quietly, behind the scenes. Think of the people you know and identify those you can serve who have nothing to offer in return. Only when we serve without expectation of personal reward do we truly follow the example of our Lord.

---

1. Krejcir, Dr. Richard J.—www.intothyword.org/apps/articles/default.asp?articleid=38075&columnid=3803
2. Ibid—www.intothyword.org/apps/articles/default.asp?articleid=38075&columnid=3803
3. King, Jr., Martin Luther—www.sptimes.com/2003/05/28/ Columns/Service_to_others_giv.shtml

6. Pray

A story to start

When they think of kings, most people think of power. But I know its limits. I am Hezekiah, King of Judah. Yesterday, I went to the temple. It was the most profound experience of my life.

The last few weeks have been horrible. A sick king is nothing more than a sick man. And I have been sick. I've been sick before, of course, but this time I thought I was going to die. In a way, I wanted to die, at least until Isaiah asked for an audience with me to give me a word from the Lord. His message? "This is God's word for you: 'Set your house in order, for you shall die, and not live.'"

As soon as the words were out of his mouth I knew that I did not want to die—not for a long time. I couldn't bear to look at anyone and turned to the wall and wept and prayed. I entreated God for more time. Oh the agony of soul as I, a king, humbled myself before God Almighty and begged for mercy as condemned men have begged me for mercy. I've seen it before. I am familiar with how it is done.

I reminded God that He had heard me before. Not long ago, Sennacherib, king of Assyria, had come against us. I prayed then—as fervently as I thought was possible—and God heard me. He sent His angel of death and killed a hundred and eighty-five thousand of my enemy's warriors in one night. Sennacherib fled back to Nineveh where he went to the temple of his gods. As he worshipped there, two of his own sons attacked him with swords and killed him.

God had heard me then when I was pleading for the nation. Now I was pleading for myself. Could He hear me? Would He answer?

I groaned. I writhed. The anguish of soul was as bad as the physical pain I suffered from the boils. Suddenly, as my strength was about gone, Isaiah returned. He said, "Before I got through the middle court on the way out, the word of the Lord came to me again. I am to tell you that God has heard your prayer and three days from now you will be well enough to go to the house of the Lord. Specifically, God is giving you fifteen more years. What's more, He's promised to protect the city during that time."

Then he called to one of my servants to bring a lump of figs. He placed it on one of the boils for a few moments. When he removed it, the boil was gone. I trembled with joy and fear. One by one, the grievous sores gave way to the power of heaven. When he was done, I was spent. This encounter with the man of God exhausted me.

Yesterday was the third day since all that happened. Sure enough, I was able to get up and go to the temple. As I worshipped God in His own house, I was overwhelmed by the experience. A few days ago, it seemed I would never enter the sacred courts again. And there I was, lifting my hands to the Lord who delivered the city and spared my life.

What are we talking about?

Prayer is sometimes seen to be nothing more than saying words without paying attention at all. Familiar prayers like "the Lord's prayer" are not the only form of this kind of prayer. A friend of mine told me how, on one occasion, he knelt beside the bed with his wife at the end of a long day. He was weary beyond belief and, unthinkingly, said, "Dear heavenly Father, we thank you for the food we are about to receive..." and was interrupted by his wife's giggle.

Mere repetition of words, however biblical they may be, is not our area of interest here. We're looking at real communication, specifically between us and God. Prayer embraces a number of distinct activities—confession of sin, asking for needs to be met, intercession for others, adoration, and thanksgiving. These are all significant and each adds its own contribution to the whole.

For our purposes we will cast the net as widely as possible and simply define prayer as spiritual communion with God.

Biblical background

We know prayer is important because of the biblical emphasis on it. We see Jesus as a man of prayer. For example, in Luke 6:12 we read of him going out to a mountain to pray all night long.

Jesus also taught about prayer. He said things like: "When you pray, you must not be like the hypocrites. For they love to stand and pray in the synagogues and at the street corners, that they may be seen by others. Truly, I say to you, they have received their reward. But when you pray, go into your room and shut the door and pray to your Father who is in secret. And your Father who sees in secret will reward you. And when you pray, do not heap up empty phrases as the Gentiles do, for they think that they will be heard for their many words" (Matt. 6:5-7 ESV).

> "...prayer is the most common complement to mainstream medicine, far outpacing acupuncture, herbs, vitamins and other alternative remedies."[1]

The apostle Paul also set an example by recording several prayers in his letters and he, too, taught about the importance of prayer, the need for prayer, and the effects of prayer. I won't even attempt to convince you that Christians should approach prayer seriously. Most of us instinctively know it, even if we would condemn ourselves regarding our diligence in practising it.

Exploring prayer

"How's your prayer life?" A friend loved to ask questions like this to make me squirm. When I had suffered enough, he said, "I've asked that question of all kinds of people and every one has expressed some kind of dissatisfaction about the quality or quantity of prayer in his or her life." This is probably true for all spiritual activities, but because we see prayer as pivotal, it serves as a lightning rod.

We take a disciplined approach to prayer for several reasons. The easiest one is to follow Christ's example and obey biblical commands. A little beneath the surface are some other reasons. Prayer allows us to engage personally with God, to practise His presence. Disciplined prayer also makes sure that time with God is not crowded out of our lives by sloth from within or urgencies from without. Most of us pray because we sense a need of some sort. When trouble comes, praying is as instinctive for the Christian, as crying is for the child. We hurt; we want God to do something about it. As we mature, though, we discover that our agenda may not fit perfectly with God's. Only after we spend a great deal of time with Him, do we internalize His values, priorities and will.

Some of us love to measure progress. We like to see positive change in our lives. We seem to need that encouragement to keep on. For those who fall into this category, we'd like to be able to evaluate our prayer life. I've learned that success in one's prayer life is not measured by the degree to which we can get God to react to people and circumstances as we see them, but the degree to which we come to react to people and circumstances the way God sees them. This is counterintuitive for most of us. Even the most godly tend to see answers to prayer only when their own will is done in their lives or the lives of others.

> "Surveys have found that perhaps half of Americans regularly pray for their own health, and at least a quarter have others pray for them. ...one of the many difficulties that critics and advocates say makes studying prayer problematic: There is no way to quantify the "dose," and no way to know whether people outside the study may be praying for its subjects, diluting the effects."

In fact, while it is not usually wrong to pray for things to go the way you would like them to, the goal in prayer is for us to get to the point where we are asking God how we can conform to His purposes in the circumstances in which we now find ourselves, even if they include things we would naturally want to avoid. We limit the benefit of the exercise if we insist on God doing what we think is best for us and those we love. We will be much better off if we let Him set the agenda and we seek to fit into it.

Over the years, I've collected some practical tips to enhance my prayer life. I hope you will find them useful.

- Be specific. God is glorified by our gratitude for the things He does for us. When we are specific in our prayers, we can see specific answers, and we'll give specific praise.
- Listen as much as you talk. One-sided conversations are singularly dissatisfying for the listener. Take time to listen for God's voice as you pray. He may have some things to say.
- Confess your sins. Sin always interferes with our intimacy with God. If you are serious about listening to God, He'll bring to your mind the sins that are getting in the way.
- Be patient. We are usually in a bigger hurry than God is. Understand that He not only has the right to answer in His time, He will answer only in His time. Timing is part of His answer.
- Use a list. A list is useful for overcoming memory weaknesses and for recording answers. Over time, as you align your will with God's, it will change from a prayer list to a praise list.
- Pray aloud. Verbalizing our prayers has real benefits. When we discipline ourselves to form words and speak them aloud, we'll find it easier to stay focussed on the things we are trying to present to the Lord.
- At the same time, do not hesitate to spend time in God's presence when you are unable to put words to whatever it is you are bringing to your Father.
- Pray for inner change. Frequent, sincere prayer

regarding the "restricted areas" of your life is crucial if you are going to become more like the Lord Jesus. Ask God to make you the person He intends for you to be.

+ Pray with faith. Faithless prayer is an oxymoron. The key here is to remember that our faith is in God, not in a specific outcome which we have decided will be best. Let God choose the best outcome. His choice will be better than ours!

Potential pitfalls

Because of our tendency to sin, even a serious approach to prayer can be tainted. This emphasis may lead to our limiting prayer to a structured time and form. But prayer needs both spontaneity and structure. We lose out if we practise one at the expense of the other. Prayer can also degenerate into the subjective ramblings of a dissatisfied soul trying to get God to give it what it wants. In some cases, prayer can also be pressed into service as a vehicle of self-promotion in the Christian community, used as nothing more than a mechanism for showing off our supposed spiritual depth in public.

A word of encouragement

I hope I've communicated that prayer is not characterized by a simple equation (as in, when I say this, God does that). Prayer is a conversation characterized by communication in both directions and a deepening of the relationship between the participants.

---

1. Rob Stein, "Researchers Look at Prayer and Healing," Washington Post, March 24, 2006

2. Ibid

7. Say "No" to Yourself

A story to start

No stronger temptation exists than to copy the behaviour of others when you find yourself alone in the enemy's territory. I am Ezra the scribe and priest to God, born as an exile in Babylon, living free in Jerusalem by the grace of God and the decrees of Cyrus and Darius. Despite efforts to the contrary, our Jewish faith was not diluted by the years of exile in a strange land.

Though far from the holy mount, though deprived of our temple, though unable to worship God with the sacrifices He ordained, we kept the faith. We studied the Torah. We laboured to understand its subtlest nuances. We rigourously followed its slightest command. We faithfully passed on its teaching.

As a righteous Jew living in the midst of unrighteous Babylon, I found the old ways to be a source of strength to resist assimilation into the pagan culture around me. The celebration of every feast day, the regular prayers, the ritual washings, the solemn fasts all reminded me of the God of my fathers who had rescued us before and would rescue us again.

From the first year of Cyrus, king of Persia, hope arose in the despondent hearts of my fellow exiles. The king's decree, moved by God Himself, launched a series of expeditions to our homeland and at last, my turn came.

As we began the journey, I sent word to the town of Casiphia, requesting some of the Levites there to join us. We had sacred temple vessels with us and it was only right that they be in the care of the sons of Levi. Some thirty-eight responded and brought their households with them.

Yet there was a worry that the temple treasure that we had with us might attract pagan plunderers who would steal and defile the holy articles which had been consecrated to God. It occurred to me to ask for an escort of soldiers to protect us. Yet we had boasted to the King: "The hand of our God blesses all who seek Him, and the almighty power of His anger is against everyone who forsakes Him." Would he not think poorly of our God if we now begged him for his military protection?

I did what had become my habit through my life. I proclaimed a fast. We denied ourselves the pleasure of eating and the strength it would give us. We made ourselves entirely vulnerable and cast ourselves upon our God. We would not turn to the strength of the king, but depend entirely on the mighty arm of God. When the period of fasting was completed, I divided the treasure among the priests and Levites and charged them with keeping it safe until our arrival in Jerusalem.

Our fasting and prayer was honoured by the God of the Universe. After three and a half months trudging through lands inhabited only by beasts and men equally untamed, we arrived at the Holy City. Meremoth, the priest, and his Levite assistants received the treasure which was delivered without the smallest loss. Once everything was counted and recorded, we went to the temple, where, for the first time in our lives, we were able to make sacrifices to God on His holy hill.

What are we talking about?

Fasting is simply abstaining from something, usually food. A fast can be complete or partial. Most fasts allow water, though some allow other clear beverages. While fasting may be used in different ways by different people, our focus is on its spiritual benefits.

Biblical background

While Christians are generally interested in fasting as a topic, few are disposed to practise it. Consider Jesus' words to the crowd: *"... when you fast, do not be like the hypocrites, with a sad countenance. For they disfigure their faces that they may appear to men to be fasting. Assuredly, I say to you, they have their reward. But you, when you fast, anoint your head and wash your face, so that you do not appear to men to be fasting, but to your Father who is in the secret place; and your Father who sees in secret will reward you openly"* (Matt. 6:16-17 NKJV). Notice that while Jesus does not command His followers to fast, He assumes that they will by His use of the phrase "when you fast."

Gentile Christians may feel that Jesus was speaking in the Jewish context and was not implying that fasting would be part of their life. In response, I point to Jesus' answer to the disciples of John. They asked Him, *"'Why do we and the Pharisees fast often, but Your disciples do not fast?' And Jesus said to them, 'Can the friends of the bridegroom mourn as long as the bridegroom is with them? But the days will come when the bridegroom will be taken away from them, and then they will fast'"* (Matt. 9:14-15 NKJV). The book of Acts indicates that fasting was part of early church practice. In 2 Corinthians, Paul referred twice to his own habit of fasting.

> *"Fasting is not an end in itself; it is a means by which we can worship the Lord and submit ourselves in humility to Him. We don't make God love us any more than He already does if we fast, or if we fast longer. Fasting invites God into the problem. Then in the strength of God, victory is possible."*[1]

Exploring fasting

Among the reasons to practise fasting, I would place following Christ's expectations and the pattern of the early church at the top of the list. Fasting allows us to sharpen our focus on God in a conscious way. The hunger pangs which we experience serve as frequent reminders that we are performing a spiritual exercise. Most of the time, even when we give thanks before eating, the satiation of hunger is just a natural part of our day without spiritual implications. Occasional fasting draws our attention to the link between God as the source of life and His role as the sustainer of life.

> **Fasting helps us to...**
> ...follow Christ's expectations (not command)
> ...sharpen our focus on God
> ...be conscious of our dependence on God
> ...be free from slavery to pleasing ourselves
> ...recognize character issues which need to be addressed

One of the great benefits of fasting is our liberation from the everyday slavery of pleasing ourselves. We are so used to thoughtlessly satisfying our physical appetites that we become habituated to the idea that these appetites must be served. Fasting reminds us that the spiritual transcends the physical.

One more benefit of fasting is its ability to raise character issues which need to be addressed. Stress usually reveals negative aspects of the inner self. Fasting is a controlled source of stress and can help us spot our weaknesses. Things like impatience, ungratefulness, and temper will become evident and we can use this awareness to grow spiritually.

Let me suggest a few practical tips regarding fasting:

- Know your spiritual goal before you start. It may be as general as desiring to humble yourself before God or as specific as seeking guidance regarding some "next step" in your life. Whatever it is, identify it before you start.
- Start small. Skip one meal to begin to get a sense of what to expect. Gradually increase your fasting time, but know why you are doing it. Just as long prayers don't impress God (Matt. 6:7), neither do long fasts.
- Check with your doctor. This is not a significant issue if you have "normal health," but fasting can be dangerous if you have health problems, particularly those related to the regulation of blood sugar.
- Consider partial fasts (especially if you have health issues). We don't fast to prove something to God

(or anyone else). Fasting from a particular food item or food group may accomplish your spiritual goals if you have the appropriate attitude.

- Break your fast with healthy, fibre-rich foods. Longer fasts may produce a strong desire for fats, salt and sugar. Avoid overindulging these cravings as you end your fast. Try a salad with whole-grain bread instead.

> *"Fasting reminds us that we are sustained 'by every word that proceeds from the mouth of God' (Matt. 4:4). Food does not sustain us; God sustains us."*[2]

- When an invitation to eat comes during your fast time, you can truthfully say, "That's not convenient for me, how about next week?" If the person needs your company or counsel and they have no time other than a meal time, break your fast. In "Wisdom of the Desert," Thomas Merton tells of two men visiting a friend on a day when he typically fasted. He enthusiastically invited them to eat with him. He reasoned that "fasting has its reward, but he who eats out of charity fulfils two commandments, for he sets aside his own will and he refreshes his hungry brethren."[3]

Potential pitfalls

In our multi-task culture, we love to combine things. I would counsel you against combining fasting with dieting. If you need to lose weight, find a healthy way to do that and stick to it faithfully. The spiritual benefit of fasting is watered down when we try to use it to attain physical results. Be careful as well not to use fasting to impress people (either others or yourself) with your spirituality or will power. It is easy to fall into that trap. The last danger of fasting I'll mention is the tendency some have to use fasting to manipulate God to do something for us. God does not "owe us" because we practise this or any other spiritual activity.

A word of encouragement

One of the questions that nearly always comes up when I talk about fasting is "What if someone finds out?" Jesus warned against making a show of fasting, so we shouldn't brag about it, but being paranoid about others finding out is not healthy either. Overemphasis on secrecy can be as much a point of pride as boasting. It's virtually impossible to hide fasting from family members and difficult to keep from workmates. Don't make a big deal about it either way. It's just something you do. People will get used to it.

In closing, I don't know any who have seriously tried fasting and wished they hadn't, but I do know some who haven't who have wondered if they've missed something.

---

1. Towns, Elmer L.—www.wcg.org/lit/spiritual/group/ discip6.htm
2. Foster, Richard J.—www.wcg.org/lit/spiritual/ group/ discip6.htm
3. Merton, Thomas—"Wisdom of the Desert: Translations from the 'Verba Seniorum,'" N.Y., New Directions Books, 1970

8. Live Simply

A story to start

Some behave eccentrically because they want to be different from the crowd. Others are deemed to be eccentric because they are different from the crowd. It seems I have always been different. My name is John Ben Zacharias, though I am commonly known as John the Baptizer.

Because my parents were already old when I was born, the demands on me were substantial. The bulk of my time was spent taking care of things they couldn't. However, I don't resent that time. My father was a priest and merely being with him was a spiritual education in itself. Sometimes, when I would glance at him, he would be looking intently at me as if trying to figure out who I was. I found this odd at first, but got used to it.

In my youth, I divided my time between caring for my increasingly needy parents and learning my duties as a priest. Little energy remained to engage in the pursuits that claimed the attention of my peers. For a while, they urged me to participate in their social enterprises, but after many sincere attempts to draw me in, they gave up.

This suited me as, quite frankly, I found their interests petty and their activities vain. I had the most profound sense that God was at work just under the surface of our troubled little nation and that at any moment He would burst in upon us. My consuming desire became to know God intimately and to be useful in the redemption of Israel.

After the death of my dear parents, my time was largely my own. I abandoned temple service because I could see that most of the priests were acting more out of self-interest than the desire to serve God. Eager ambitious young men jostling for position rendered my absence from the rotation inconsequential.

I went for long walks in the wilderness. Sometimes, I would walk so far that I had to spend the night out there. As the years passed, the wilderness became my second home. Eventually, I can tell you, it became my first home. I felt closest to God when I was in the great expanse of the semi-desert far from the distractions of human society.

As time passed, things which once seemed essential became unnecessary. I learned that God even provides free food in the wilderness. My needs became less and less as I became more and more convinced that the only thing that mattered was following God's call. For the last few years, I have owned only the rough clothes I make for myself and the stout staff I carry to discourage occasional wild animals and to support me when I climb in the high places.

I speak of repentance to all who will listen. I go down to the Jordan River where people come to refresh themselves. There, I preach repentance to the pleasure seekers who have settled for lesser things and missed the greatest pleasure of all, the presence of God. Some laugh and mock the "mad man" on the other side of the river. Most just sit there torn between their love for God and their love of trivial things. A few add their tears to the waters of the Jordan as they try to join me on the other side. One day, I came down into the water myself and so began my ministry of baptism.

Then yesterday, it happened. As expected, God broke through in the most amazing way. My cousin, Jesus, arrived as I preached and the Spirit of God within me showed me He is the Messiah. As children I had spent time with the Anointed One. I was overcome by the privilege I had, not being able to recognize at the time I was enjoying it.

I proclaimed Him immediately—the Lamb of God who takes away the sin of the world. Again the crowd responded with the same mix of disbelief, inner tension, and faith. Something significant is about to happen and I am so glad to be here to see it.

What are we talking about?

Simplicity is a lifestyle of reduced needs. It is related to frugality but differs in that frugality involves the minimal expenditure of money, while simplicity involves learning to want less. (A frugal person may invest much effort figuring a way to have what he or she wants without spending money for it, perhaps by bartering or building, while the simple person doesn't want it at all.)

Biblical background

Simplicity challenges the ethos of our culture. Jesus spoke up in opposition to the malady of material madness with these words: *"Do not lay up for yourselves treasures on earth, where moth and rust destroy and where thieves break in and steal, but lay up for yourselves treasures in heaven, where neither moth nor rust destroys and where thieves do not break in and steal. For where your treasure is, there your heart will be also"* (Matt. 6:19-21 ESV). Jesus leaves no doubts about Kingdom priorities.

Exploring simplicity

Western culture is characterized by complexity. Many of us juggle several jobs. Our families deal with a variety of interests, activities and responsibilities. The blending of families complicates our relationships. The acquisition of new material possessions forces us to store or throw out yesterday's treasures. Global issues affect us locally. Technology is exploding. Time and space seem to be shrinking. Life, itself, is becoming more and more complicated.

"He who owns little is little owned."[1]

In his book "Wisdom of the Desert: Translations from the 'Verba Seniorum,'" Thomas Merton records that "Abbot Agatho frequently admonished his disciple, saying: 'Never acquire for yourself anything that you might hesitate to give to your brother if he asked you for it, for thus you would be found a transgressor of God's command. If anyone asks, give it to him, and if anyone wants to borrow from you, do not turn away from him.'"[1]

This is one of the most divisive things you might try in your spiritual life. In every family, some members passionately acquire and store things, while others use them, then pass them along and be rid of them. I've seen this tension in many families, including my own. Finding a balance everyone can live with is a challenge.

> "The cost of a thing is the amount of... life which is required to be exchanged for it, immediately or in the long run."[2]

Applied to time and activities as well as space and possessions, simplicity brings many benefits. It can free us from the bondage of busyness. Most people I know complain of the pace of life and all the obligations they feel compelled to juggle. The fact is, some, if not most, of the obligations are the result of choices. If we had the will to do it, most of us could at least cut back on our activities.

Living simply can also free us from the bondage of things. When necessity demands it, we can get by with remarkably few material possessions. Too many of us live in voluntary slavery to the things that we own. The more we accumulate, the more time we have to invest in using them, maintaining them and justifying our having them. Once again, if we have the will to divest ourselves of the "stuff" in our lives, we can do it.

Living simply allows us to be much better stewards of the earth and our portion of its resources. In the end, nothing is "ours" so we should hesitate to consider ourselves anything more than stewards of the resources God has placed in our hands. When we use more than we need, we deprive others of their share. We also deplete raw materials and contribute to pollution.

Living a simple life with minimal physical possessions allows us to focus the use of our resources on the work of God. Most of the "stuff" we have is not necessary for us to do what God asks us to do. We get it because it amuses us, comforts us, pleasures us... in other words, it becomes all about us. Letting go of those superfluous things gives us time to focus on doing what God wants us to do with our lives.

As we live a simpler life, we'll find more time to enjoy what God has given us and, instead of being in bondage to it, we can be thankful for it. God will give us everything we need to do what He asks us to do. When we limit ourselves to that, we explore new levels of joy and contentment. A friend of mine who is a refugee in Canada and has next to nothing of this world's things nearly always replies "content" to questions about how he is doing... and he means that. His answer reflects the reality of a soul at rest. Why would you want to be merely "fine" when you could be "content?"

Simplicity helps us to...
...*free ourselves from the bondage of busyness*
...*free ourselves from the bondage of things*
...*be good stewards of the earth and our portion of its resources*
...*focus the use of our resources on the work of God*
...*give ourselves time to enjoy what God has given us and be thankful for it*
...*remind ourselves that we don't "deserve" more, newer, better, etc.*
...*take positive action against the materialism we so frequently decry*
...*learn that God is enough*

Choosing simplicity reminds us that we don't somehow "deserve" more, newer, better, regardless of what the commercials and advertisements try to communicate to us. Imagine being free from what seems to have become the obligation of responding to every message about "new and improved" products of every kind. In our culture, we often feel somehow as if we are missing the mark if we don't buy the latest and best version of everything. This is particularly true in the computing/electronics field. It is embarrassing to have version 14.6 once 15.0 is released.

Finally, simplicity refocusses and heads us in the direction of learning that God is enough. Here are some words of the apostle Paul. Note particularly his use of the phrase "with a continual lust for more." It is so characteristic of people who have not learned that God is enough. *"So I tell you,"* writes Paul, *"and insist on it in the Lord, that you must no longer live as the Gentiles do, in the futility of their thinking. They are darkened in their understanding and separated from the life of God because of the ignorance that is in them due to the hardening of their hearts. Having lost all sensitivity, they have given themselves over to sensuality so as to indulge in every kind of impurity, with a continual lust for more"* (Eph. 4:17-19 NIV).

"The chase after a wealthy life style is a rather complicated affair: the standards keep shifting, and the worries are many. That's why Christian contemplatives and mystics speak so often of 'detachment'. By taking our focus off of getting stuff, we have more of ourselves available to focus on learning to love rightly, or taking time to be face-to-face with those in need, or learning Scripture, or learning how to depend on the Spirit. You can't follow Christ and chase wealth; most of the time, the paths go in opposite directions."[3]

This passage deals principally with immoral behaviour for which those who indulge themselves have a "continual lust for more." But this is true for all indulgences. Those who give in to the ambition to acquire and possess are equally bound by the "continual lust for more."

Potential pitfalls

In the interest of full disclosure, I confess to being unable to identify one specific pitfall which is associated with simple living. Of course, the general ones are all hovering in the background, so as you commit to living simply, watch out for pride, a legalistic spirit, and the general air of superiority over others—which feels so good to us and completely negates any benefit from the spiritual exercise which we practise with such commitment.

A word of encouragement

To practise simplicity, plan your day with simplicity in mind. Schedule leisure time into your day, but identify time wasted on things that truly don't matter. Guard your mind from clutter as well as your home. Junk ideas will prompt you to fill your life with junk things. Take an inventory of your resources, including your time, money, talent and energy. Note how these things are being invested. Look at your things. Identify the luxuries—things that are not necessary for basic sustenance of a healthy life. As you identify them, ask yourself:

> Guard your mind from clutter as well as your home. Junk ideas will prompt you to fill your life with junk things.

- ✦ Was the resource investment needed to acquire this worth it?
- ✦ How would God have me use this now that I have it?
- ✦ Would God have me dispose of this to make my life simpler?

In the future, think twice, buy once. The bigger the purchase, the longer you should spend deciding if you need it. Ask hard questions about the motives behind the desire for the things you want. Pay more attention to "needs" and less to "wants."

---

1. Thoreau, Henry David—http://www.ehow.com/how_111392_buy-nothing.html
2. Thoreau, Henry David—http://www.quotationspage.com/quote/27136.html
3. Merton, Thomas—"Wisdom of the Desert: Translations from the 'Verba Seniorum,'" quoted at watersedge

9. Sacrifice Yourself

A story to start

To bring joy to the heart of others is one of the highest callings of God. To fulfill this calling is to experience unimaginable joy. At least, that is my personal observation. I am Epaphroditus.

Our church in Philippi began with a handful of people: Lydia and her household along with a few of her friends who met regularly for prayer, the city jailer with his household, and just a few others. By their faithful words and acts of compassion, they drew others of us to the faith and we began to walk in the way of Jesus.

We always had a great regard for Paul. His visit was used by God to bring the first converts together. We have never forgotten this and we all see him as our spiritual father. When we heard that he had been transferred to a prison in Rome, our hearts went out to him. The jailer described conditions there. Rome did not provide for the physical needs of her prisoners and we knew Paul's friends would have to rally around him. We counted ourselves among those who would have to supply his needs.

Together we were thrilled at how the Spirit of God opened our hearts and our purses. The saints didn't just give a few coins left over after they met their own needs. They gave generously. They deprived themselves, so that the gift to Paul could be an abundant one. Particularly moving were the gifts given by the slaves among us. Some had been carefully saving what tiny amounts they could to buy their freedom. This they brought forward to add to the collection – giving up their own freedom for their brother in chains.

At last, the collection phase was finished. What joy filled our hearts to be able to participate in this noble cause. But our task had barely begun. We still had to get this gift to Paul. The journey to Rome would take seven weeks. Even though reduced to the smallest number of most valuable coins, the gift was somewhat cumbersome. And there were dangers to consider. Such a purse would be a target for thievery. And then, once the bearer of the gift got to Rome, asking the specific whereabouts of a man charged with a capital offence may well raise questions.

I feel awkward mentioning this, but I was the one chosen to carry the sacrificial gift to Paul. I'm not sure of all the reasons, but my size probably had something to do with it. Time prohibits details of the journey. Perhaps on another occasion?

My time with Paul has been the highlight of my life. To see our old friend confined and guarded was a trial at first, but I soon learned that he had not been bowed by his captivity. What a man! He was overwhelmed with the gift. He knows our church so well. He knows we are not a wealthy group. He wept openly to think of what his brothers and sisters had given up to provide for his needs. He immediately began to compose a letter expressing his gratitude.

I didn't expect to be the one to deliver it, since I was committed to staying with Paul indefinitely as my personal gift to him, but I fell gravely ill. Even Paul thought I was going to die. However, I did recover. As soon as I was well enough to travel, Paul asked me to return home with the letter. He wanted me to be able to give a first hand report and to prove that I had not, in fact, died. (Rumours had begun to circulate!)

Yesterday, I read Paul's letter to the church and then we stayed up past midnight as they asked question after question. We were all joyfully exhausted as we parted. God had used us to share in His work through His servant. We were content.

What are we talking about?

The concept of sacrifice flows in two parallel channels – the specific and the general. Specifically, "sacrifice" refers to the offering of a life (usually animal and typically by fire) to appease or honour a deity. Generally, it means giving up something highly prized or an advantage of some sort for the benefit of another person. In our consideration of the topic, we'll focus on the general aspect of giving up something of value in order to benefit someone else and notice that this kind of selfless act is glorifying to God at the same time.

Biblical background

Turning to the Bible, I'll choose just one passage to serve as a background: Mark 12:41 to 44 where we read that Jesus *"sat down opposite the treasury and watched the people putting money into the offering box. Many rich people put in large sums. And a poor widow came and put in two small copper coins, which make a penny. And he called his disciples to him and said to them, 'Truly, I say to you, this poor widow has put in more than all those who are contributing to the offering box. For they all contributed out of their abundance, but she out of her poverty has put in everything she had, all she had to live on'"* (Mark 12:41-44 ESV).

This passage reminds us that it is not the size of the sacrifice that makes it valuable, but the spirit which stimulates it. Sacrifice, such as the widow's, moves us into experiencing true dependence on God. It is one thing to give what we don't need. It is another to relinquish that on which we depend ourselves. Read the biographies of some of the missionaries of the early and mid 1800s. Some gave up literal fortunes and profitable careers and casting themselves entirely on God went off into the unknown. Many sacrificed their health, relationships, even their own lives because they believed the furthering of God's purposes on earth was worth far more than anything else known to humanity.

Exploring sacrifice

In the first half of the 20th Century, Canadians rallied to the cry "For God, King, and Country." Those were the priorities for which they were prepared to make the sacrifice of going to war and, if called upon, to give up their lives. In 2010, MacLean's Magazine published the response to a new poll asking what Canadians would be willing to die for. Permitted more than one choice, 83% said they would die for their family, 32% for their country, and 28% for their God. (See MacLean's[1]) While a sacrificial death for the benefit of others is honourable and laudable, in some ways a sacrificial life may be even more of a challenge.

In the Old Testament, sacrifice nearly always spoke of the offering of animals. In an agrarian culture, giving up the best of your herd or flock was a powerful picture of your regard for God and your dependence on Him. In those days before multinational seed companies, farmers typically would keep the best of their crops and herds for seeding or breeding. This ensured the maintenance of the highest possible quality for future generations. So offering your best to God was a practical sacrifice as well as a symbolic expression of faith.

Ancient Israelites expressed their trust in God every time they gave up a choice animal as a sacrifice. Defective animals were never acceptable as sacrifices and several passages in the Old Testament reveal God's anger at being given left overs and cast offs.

Since God's satisfaction with the once-for-all sacrifice of Jesus, animal sacrifices have been set aside. Most of us don't even own flocks or herds, but we all have things we value. In our culture, we usually think of material wealth symbolized by money, investments, property or possessions. But serious Christians should consider that God would welcome the sacrifice of some intangibles like time, skills, privacy, and reputation.

> **Sacrifice helps us to...**
> ...experience true dependence on God for more than just finances; it can touch your comfort, sleep, privacy, reputation, career, safety or anything else you prize
> ...experience God's miraculous provision
> ...move us out of our material "comfort zone"
> ...surrender our hopes and dreams for earthly or material fulfillment in favour of spiritual, intangible, future blessings

Sacrifice Yourself

Earlier, we talked about simplicity. Let me mention that sacrifice differs from simplicity in that simplicity only touches the things we call "extras" or "luxuries." Sacrifice digs deeper and calls us to share things we truly need and will have to do without unless God makes up the difference.

As I hinted a moment ago, true sacrifice will involve more than just finances. It can touch your comfort, sleep, privacy, reputation, career, safety or anything else you value highly. It is not only financial sacrifice which stimulates God's miraculous provision. He will also supply energy, strength, comfort and whatever else we need when we leave Easy Street behind along with its dreams for earthly or material fulfilment in favour of the Narrow Way with its spiritual, intangible, and mostly future blessings.

Potential pitfalls

It is only fair to mention that like everything else we can do to enhance our spiritual life, sacrifice has its own potential pitfalls. Sacrifice can be used to legitimize irresponsibility. It can also be pressed into service to test or to manipulate God. We think to ourselves, "If I give up this cherished thing, God will have to give me this other thing that I want." Not so. We delude ourselves. Such a thing is not sacrifice at all, but an attempt to control. What we surrender in exchange for material benefit, honour, gratitude, or social influence is not worthy of being called "sacrifice."

A word of encouragement

So how can we get started? Well, examine your values and sources of security. Sacrifice will cost you, so look at the things you prize most highly. Identify some things you would be prepared to sacrifice. Remember, it need not be financial. It might be the time required to learn a skill you'd like to have, or the comfort of staying in your own cozy home when there are people on the street to whom you could minister. Then, ask God to show you something He wants you to trust Him for – exclusively. If you are honest about your desire to sacrifice, God will show you what He wants. Pray that He would open your heart to the needs around you—and they are all around you. Then, prepare yourself psychologically by identifying the needs in your environment. Think about what it would take to meet those needs even partially. When you find a correlation between a need and your resources, do something about it. Finally, don't hang around waiting to be thanked.

---

1. www.macleans.ca/article.jsp?content=20040607_81769_81769 (Source: Pollara)

10. Be Generous

A story to start

It's odd how reputations get started and stick. It's somewhat embarrassing when that reputation is built on a recognized virtue while the one who owns it is painfully aware of his shortcomings and has an entirely different perspective on things. I am Joseph, the one nicknamed "Barnabas."

I didn't intend to stand out from the crowd. Others were doing no less than I did. The new fellowship of believers in Jesus, the Messiah, was struggling to establish itself in Jerusalem and I had a property which I had little interest in and no time for. It only made sense to turn it into cash and invest it in support of something I had great interest in and gave all of my available time to.

It gave me great pleasure to give the proceeds of the sale of my field to the apostles. One of them said, "Joseph, dear brother, you are a great encouragement to the whole church in Jerusalem." Next thing I knew I was being called "Barnabas" the son of encouragement. In short order, it seemed my given name was abandoned in favour of this nickname.

I feel odd about being credited with something which is part of my nature and part of the work of the Holy Spirit. I can't say I ever had to work very hard at developing a generous streak. I was never what anyone would call "a wealthy man" and once that field was sold I had little of value except my time. So I used that to help my brothers and sisters. I loved to invest my time in discipling them in the ways of Jesus, helping them grow toward spiritual maturity.

I take no small satisfaction in my influence on Paul. When I began working with him, he still reeked of his pharisaical background. The eradication of that particular "quality" was a source of many private chuckles and great joy for me. (Though I was always careful to not discourage or embarrass him, even privately.) How he struggled to let go of the law and embrace grace! I feared he'd never really get it. Let me quickly confess that his victory in this regard certainly wasn't all due to my efforts with him, but I'm glad that God used me to play a part in his development.

While my relationship with Paul was among the things which brought me the most pleasure in my life, it also brought me the most pain. I can't begin to describe my sorrow concerning that row we had over John Mark. (Some of those heated conversations still linger in my memory, though I harbour no grudge or ill will.) My intention was to do for that young man nothing more nor less than what I had done for Paul, himself.

I could see great gifts in him and wanted to expose him to the inner circles of leadership in the church where he might be noticed and given a chance to exercise his gifts. Somehow Paul had forgotten the process of his own rise to a place of significant ministry influence. Maybe he saw his own weaknesses reflected in John Mark and that increased his negative feelings. Who on earth, but the Spirit of God, knows such things?

That's all behind us now. Though we parted company over it a long time ago and lost the benefit of years of fellowship, God was generous and gave us both a measure of blessing for our labours. Paul's renown has increased with his travels and now Luke has started writing about the development of the church. That work contains a lot of biographical material about Paul and the associates he invited to join him.

I'm content to have poured a few more years into John Mark. I can't tell you how gratified I was when word filtered out from Timothy that Paul had requested Mark to come to Rome to minister to him. I also understand that my name appears in some of the letters Paul has written to the churches. I guess he learned more about generosity than I thought he might.

As for myself, even though I know my best years are behind me, I've taken note of another young man I'd like to put some time into.

What are we talking about?

Generosity involves giving and, because of that, is closely linked to simplicity and sacrifice. It highlights liberality, freedom from stingy or miserly impulses, extending beyond the minimum to meet the immediate need and reaching into the realm of abundance, even excess.

"Real generosity is doing something nice for someone who will never find out."[1]

Biblical background

The Bible has quite a bit to say about generosity. Starting in the Old Testament, we find God's people urged to be generous in giving to the Lord. In Exodus, we read: *"Take from among you a contribution to the* LORD. *Whoever is of a generous heart, let him bring the* LORD'*s contribution"* (Ex. 35:5 ESV). Then lest anyone be unsure about just what might be considered worthy, we find a list starting with gold, silver, and bronze; and including the finest textiles, furs, woods, and precious stones.

The New Testament builds on the Old Testament's emphasis on generosity in giving material things. It includes those but challenges us to be generous with our love as well. *"Give to everyone who begs from you, and from one who takes away your goods do not demand them back. And as you wish that others would do to you, do so to them. If you love those who love you, what benefit is that to you? For even sinners love those who love them. And if you do good to those who do good to you, what benefit is that to you? For even sinners do the same. And if you lend to those from whom you expect to receive, what credit is that to you? Even sinners lend to sinners, to get back the same amount. But love your enemies, and do good, and lend, expecting nothing in return, and your reward will be great, and you will be sons of the Most High, for he is kind to the ungrateful and the evil. Be merciful, even as your Father is merciful"* (Luke 6:30-36 ESV).

Other passages highlight God's generosity in offering salvation to sinners: Jesus told His followers, *"I came that they may have life and have it abundantly"* (John 10:10 ESV). Paul wrote *"If, because of one man's trespass, death reigned through that one man, much more will those who receive the abundance of grace and the free gift of righteousness reign in life through the one man Jesus Christ"* (Rom. 5:17 ESV). Then later in the same letter, he included this practical advice for Christians: *"Having gifts that differ according to the grace given to us, let us use them: if prophecy, in proportion to our faith; if service, in our serving; the one who teaches, in his teaching; the one who exhorts, in his exhortation; the one who contributes, in generosity; the one who leads, with zeal; the one who does acts of mercy, with cheerfulness"* (Rom. 12:6-8 ESV).

Exploring generosity

John Wesley, the English evangelist, is credited with this bit of advice to Christians:

> "Do all the good you can,
> By all the means you can,
> In all the ways you can,
> In all the places you can,
> At all the times you can,
> To all the people you can,
> As long as ever you can."[2]

Johann Wolfgang von Goethe, the great German writer, suggested: "Be generous with kindly words, especially about those who are absent."

Here's a great little thought as we get started. I don't have the author's name, but it appeared on the Whitestone Journal website: "This is almost funny, in a sad way. Nearly all of us have the illusion that 'my time is my own.' It isn't. Everything belongs to God, and He is very generous with time. We are given a good deal of it, and expected to make a return. When we say we don't have time for reading Scripture, or volunteering, or for children, we are telling a lie. We all waste time. If we used all the wasted time in a fruitful way, we would be far more effective. The first step to being generous with time is to acknowledge that our time is not our own, it is a gift from God. And it was meant to be shared."[3]

> **Being generous helps us to...**
> ...live out the expression of God's grace in our own life
> ...bless others
> ...stimulate thanksgiving and worship
> ...free ourselves from the human tendency to hoard

Among the many good reasons to practise generosity, we find the opportunity to bless others. What a privilege that is. So many are concerned with the flow of energy from others to themselves. They are quick to notice when others are not contributing to their well-being and happiness. A generous spirit is more concerned with the flow in the other direction. Because of that, it allows us to live out the expression of God's grace in our own life.

As Jesus said, *"Freely you have received, freely give"* (Matt. 10:8 NIV). When we give generously to others, especially if we do so anonymously, we stimulate thanksgiving and worship.

> *"Generosity consists not the sum given, but the manner in which it is bestowed."*[4]

I can't count the occasions when unexpected blessings of all kinds have provoked words of praise to pop out of my mouth, sometimes most unexpectedly. And, before I forget, generosity frees us from the human tendency to hoard. While some of us struggle with this more than others, I've come to see it as one of those weaknesses that is "a matter of degree."

Here are a few practical tips to get you started:

- At first you may need to plan to be generous (especially if you tend to be a hoarder).
- Set a practical goal concerning generous acts. The aim is to avoid being irresponsible while blessing others to the full potential God has given you.

- We'll deal with secrecy another time, but try being generous in secret so you don't become driven to receive gratitude. There is a freedom and a joy in giving anonymously, although, admittedly, it's not natural to give to others without any expectations at all—even gratitude.
- Remember to be generous with your time and attention as well as your finances and possessions. Sometimes people need us more than things we can give to them.

There's one last point which is hard, especially for those of us who are focussed on "doing." Don't forget to be generous with those closest to you. Many of us fail when it comes time to being generous at home. Plan to be generous to those you claim to love.

Potential Pitfalls

In the rush to be generous, it is possible to behave irresponsibly in regard to legitimate obligations. We live in a credit crazy culture, but I can't think of a situation in which it would be wise to find ourselves indebted in order to be generous. If you're flat out of financial resources, be generous with your time, abilities, or existing possessions.

Generosity can also run amok if we start being generous with things which belong to others. I'm thinking particularly of family resources here. It is possible for a parent to shortchange his or her children by undue generosity. Family members have a reasonable claim on all shared resources. Be as generous as you want to be with that for which you have stewardship, but avoid shortchanging others in order to be generous.

A word of encouragement

Of all the things we might do as humans which make us a little like God, being generous has to be near the top of the list.

Be Generous

Because we are not God, who enjoys infinite resources, we're aware that anything we give away diminishes or deprives us in some way. In the material world, that's true, but in the spiritual realm, we are connected to God, Himself, the source of life. His resources do not diminish as He pours out His blessing on us. He always has a full supply.

I like to use a simple illustration to help people see this. On our farm, we have both a cistern and a well. When I take water from the cistern, there is less water left behind. If I keep taking water out, eventually it will be empty. When I take water from the well (a ninety footer directly into an aquifer), it is not depleted. It's plugged into the earth's hydrological system. I pumped water from that well for four weeks straight as I filled our farm pond and never ran out. It is clear that the underground supply of water is replenished far faster than I can pull it out with a pump and hose.

If you take advantage of every opportunity to generously bless those around you in non-material ways, others will see the light of the Father shining through your eyes.

---

1. Clark, Frank A.—http://thinkexist.com/quotation/real-generosity-is-doing-something-nice-for/406611.html
2. Wesley, John—http://thinkexist.com/quotation/do_all_the_good_you_can-by_all_the_means_you_can/148152.html
3. Unknown—http://whitestonejournal.com/index.php/articles-index/38-articles/173-generosity
4. Unknown—http://www.wow4u.com/qgenerosity/index.html

11. Keep Some Secrets

A story to start

Many dream of what it would be like to be born into a rich powerful family. A few even fantasize about being a child of royalty. I doubt they ever consider the pressure of such privilege. Do they imagine themselves torn between loyal devotion to a madman and treasonous fidelity to a friend? I have walked this path. I am Jonathan, son of Saul, friend of David.

David was more than a brother to me. After my father brought him to court, we became the best of friends. As teenagers, we enjoyed months of carefree companionship. We particularly enjoyed sharpening the skills of combat together. Both of us will carry a few scars to our grave because of the sharpness of our competitions, but they were worth it.

My father's behaviour was growing ever stranger. He suffered from insomnia. He would fly into violent rages, though unprovoked by anything anyone else could see. He grew sullen and reclusive. Unthreatened, he doubled his personal guard. He would call for singers or dancers and then, before they were finished, make them flee with shouts of displeasure. He insisted that a spear always be at hand. He would hurl it at any unfortunate one who might cross him.

For me, the breaking point came the day David was playing his ten-stringed harp for my father. Though David performed for him daily, on this occasion he was called as the day was barely breaking. The king had not slept all night tormented by his fears. David launched into a ballad about the exploits of a king in battle. I suppose it brought another song to my father's mind—the one about Saul having killed his thousands and David his ten thousands. It had been sung by the maidens who did nothing to hide their admiration for the young hero.

In an explosion of rage, the King hurled his ever-present spear at David. It was only his lightning reflexes that saved his life. As my father roared for him to stay, David fled to the field where we often met in mock battle. I met him there and pledged my friendship to him regardless of what it would cost me.

As the days passed, my father's mood swings became more unsettling. No one knew what to expect from moment to moment. Sometimes he would speak of David with great warmth and admiration, but I could no longer trust him. I would make excuses for my friend and keep his whereabouts secret. On one occasion, I was the target of my father's rage and spear.

After that, it was just a matter of time. Sometimes, I knew where David was, sometimes not. I never told my father one way or the other. I ceased speaking of my friend. I didn't want to draw attention to him because my father's hatred was so consuming. Every time David's name came up, he would begin to obsessively plan for his capture and execution.

Today things are not looking good. My father's enemies have taken advantage of his being distracted by David and have assembled a large army. When the messenger arrived with the news, my father reluctantly broke off the search for David to respond to this national threat. So, for now, we are turning our attention to them.

No doubt the fighting will be fierce and my brothers and I must be at our father's side for this battle. To do less would be disloyal, if not cowardly. Personally, I doubt things will go well. We've had little time to prepare and we march to Gilboa tomorrow. My one confidence as we prepare to leave is that somewhere in the south Judean hills, my friend lies safely in secret.

What are we talking about?

Secrecy involves keeping something hidden or concealed. In its most benign form, it is simply not revealing something. There's nothing particularly sinister about not telling your friends what you bought them for their birthday. Even if they ask you what it is, you are under no moral obligation to reveal it. But secrets quickly move from this stage to demanding deception and eventually outright lying to protect them. When those who have the moral right to know start asking specific questions, we'll have to choose between protecting the secret with lies (bad choice) or speaking the truth (good choice). Because of this, secrecy has an air of suspicion about it. The questions may be asked "Why must this secret be kept?" "Is this secret legitimate, or is it hiding moral evil?"

The kind of secrecy at stake here is entirely righteous and pleasing to God and thus counter-cultural. It goes beyond keeping quiet to protect someone else's well-being or life. It protects us from the praise of other people so that we might enjoy God's praise. When we bless others secretly, the gratitude engendered in their hearts flows straight to God. Our human pride is held in check. People don't get an exalted impression of us. God is glorified. What could be better than that?

> When we bless others secretly, the gratitude engendered in their hearts flows straight to God. Our human pride is held in check. People don't get an exalted impression of us. God is glorified. What could be better than all that?

Biblical background

The single most powerful expression of the kind of secrecy that enhances our spiritual life came straight from the mouth of the Lord Jesus Christ when He said: *"Beware of practising your righteousness before other people in order to be seen by them, for then you will have no reward from your Father who is in heaven. Thus, when you give to the needy, sound no trumpet before you, as the hypocrites do in the synagogues and in the streets, that they may be praised by others. Truly, I say to you, they have received their reward. But when you give to the needy, do not let your left hand know what your right hand is doing, so that your giving may be in secret. And your Father who sees in secret will reward you"* (Matt. 6:1-4 ESV).

Few other passages deal with this topic directly. Others, having to do more with humility, support this practice but this is sufficient to establish biblical precedence for the idea of employing secrecy as a way to glorify God above all.

Exploring secrecy

With the exception of surprise birthday parties and Christmas presents, usually people consider secrecy necessary only when something has gone wrong in some way. But secrecy can be a virtue when it is used to divert attention to God instead of to ourselves. This is contrary to our usual inclinations, but aligns perfectly with true spirituality.

The natural human tendency is to practise secrecy in regard to our sin and transparency about our virtues. The more spiritually mature find this natural tendency turned on its head. As we grow into the likeness of Jesus, we will tend to emphasize the importance of secrecy about anything which might bring us the approval, adulation, honour, and recognition of the crowd. This is not the way to "get ahead in the world," but it is sure to anchor us firmly in "Kingdom culture." Along with the rest of the 19 things discussed in this book, it underscores the difference between the Kingdom of God and the kingdom of this world.

> *The natural human tendency is to practise secrecy in regard to our sin and transparency about our virtues.*

Several things stimulate the true follower of Christ to practise secrecy. First, it allows us to experience freedom from the need for human approval. This is a crucial issue in our culture where "getting credit" and "avoiding blame" are the two big factors in social advancement. These are so important that many fall to the temptation of seeking credit for accomplishments not their own and engaging in outright deception to avoid taking responsibility for their failings. Secrecy weans us from the value system that "legitimizes" these kinds of sins.

Keep Some Secrets

Jesus clearly indicated that when we do things to be noticed, and we are noticed, then we have had our reward. With this in mind, we might practise secrecy to discover the true motives for our behaviour.

- Do we do good so others will admire us?
- Do we give so others will see us as generous?
- Do we pray so others will consider us spiritual?

Secrecy also helps us to learn that we are loved because God chooses to love us, not because of our ability to perform. Some Christians confuse God's acceptance and love with the approval and appreciation of the people they serve. If people don't know that I was the one who blessed them, they will not thank me, which clears up this potential confusion – a confusion, I would contend, to which people who serve are particularly subject.

Secrecy is not so much about results as it is about motivation. Acts of kindness and sacrifice are likely to be noticed at some level. Some can't help but be observed, by the beneficiary if by no one else. The key question is "Would I do these acts if I knew there was no chance they would be noticed?" That will show you something about yourself.

Secrecy helps us to...
...experience freedom from the need for human approval
...discover the true motives for our behaviour
...learn that we are loved because God chooses to love us, not because of our ability to perform
...learn how to love people as God does—without a test of worthiness or expectation of return
...experience freedom from mutual back scratching
...stimulate thanksgiving and worship

Some other questions you might want to ask yourself as you explore your motives are:

- Am I disappointed when nobody seems to notice my current efforts?
- Am I frustrated when my past efforts are forgotten or ignored?
- Am I upset when someone else gets the credit for my ideas or accomplishments?
- Am I bothered when no one adequately expresses gratitude for my efforts?
- Am I motivated to do things so others will think I am spiritual, talented, clever, and so on?

Though practising secrecy prompts us to do good without recognition, we need not mislead or deceive people. If our motives are pure, God is honoured.

Potential Pitfalls

Watch out for a couple of potential pitfalls associated with secrecy. Satan loves to twist our best motives and actions to strip them of any spiritual benefit. When he does this, he deceives us into serving him in his rebellion against God. It's sad to think that Christians who start out with pure hearts and clean hands can have their minds deceived and their efforts perverted so that they end up actually working against their stated objectives.

In light of the above, avoid becoming paranoid about anyone finding out about your spiritual exercise. The object is simply to avoid drawing unnecessary attention to our service. When we become obsessed with keeping the good we do secret, we can fall in a couple of ways. Firstly, self-obsession is to be avoided at all costs (it is one of Satan's favourite ways of derailing believers) and, secondly, we can move beyond mere secrecy to overt misrepresentation. While our motives may be righteous, we err when we use the devil's tools to do God's work. Our objective should be nothing more than to deflect credit to God. After all, He is the one who gives us everything. If He gives us the grace to share with someone who has less, then He should get the credit and be thanked accordingly.

A word of encouragement

Secrecy plays a positive role in teaching us how to love people as God does—without a test of worthiness or expectation of return. It lets us experience freedom from the spirit of mutual back scratching which is so common. Best of all, secrecy stimulates thanksgiving and worship. When people are blessed, they instinctively desire to express gratitude. If they know the human agent of that blessing, they thank that person directly. If they don't know the human agent, then all of their appreciation is expressed to God. When God is most glorified, we are most blessed.

12. Be Open

A story to start

My connections with members of the trade guilds of Thyatira made me familiar with a closed way of living. The people with whom I did business were always fearful of outsiders stealing their trade secrets and often engaged in disgusting spiritual rituals as part of the way they protected themselves. I could never take part for, though I didn't know Him at the time, God had opened my heart to Himself. I am Lydia, seller of purple, resident of Philippi.

My growing network of clients made it worth moving from Thyatira to set up shop in Philippi which sees a lot of traffic, especially Romans, passing to and fro on commercial and military business. They use my brilliant dyes on their clothes to flaunt their wealth and status on formal occasions, so this is the perfect spot for me to do business.

One of the first things I did as soon as I arrived was to begin building a social network. I have chosen my friends carefully here because I'm an oddity—a rich unmarried woman who has abandoned traditional worship of the pantheon of gods to worship the one true God, though I didn't come to know Him personally until after I got here.

Let me tell you what I have been eagerly telling everyone else about. One day, with a handful of friends, I went down to a quiet place by the river to pray. As a group of women engaged in religious practice in a secluded spot, we would be left uninterrupted. At least normally we would.

On this particular day, we were seated in a circle on the grass, one by one imploring this God we didn't know personally to reveal Himself. Focussed as we were, we usually didn't notice passers-by on the road, but on this occasion, we became uncomfortably aware of a few men approaching uncommonly close.

They say that "time runs fast in Philippi" and in this case, I'd have to agree. These were Jewish travellers who were looking for a quiet place to pray. They had bumped into the husband of one of our little group who told them to go down to the river where they'd find some women praying. It would have been rude to refuse their request to join us and shortly we were glad they had. As soon as they began to pray, we sensed they knew the God we were seeking.

When we finished, I asked Paul, the leader of the group, to tell us about this Jesus in whose name they had been praying. To make a short story even shorter, my heart, which as I told you earlier God had already opened, immediately resonated with this truth I had been waiting for.

I declared my faith and Paul immediately explained about water baptism. I had always been leery of religious practices before, but somehow this was something I wanted to do. Right away. I sent Miri, my servant girl, home for a change of clothes and to invite the other members of my house to join us.

Paul kept talking. He could out-talk anyone I'd ever met. He was still at it when my whole household returned. I asked Paul to tell them all about Jesus while I withdrew to prepare myself for baptism. What a thrill it was to find that God had worked in their hearts as well. We were all baptized together. This was easily the best day of my life.

Amid a lot of laughter and rejoicing, we made our way back to the villa. I invited Paul and his friends to use some of the empty rooms during their stay in Philippi. After a quick consultation, they accepted my offer.

The next few days saw my business neglected as we spent virtually all of our waking hours learning everything we could about Jesus. What a thrill it was to finally know the One who had drawn my heart to Himself. What a joy it was to open my home to His servants and benefit from their wisdom. What a comfort it was to know that the Christian faith was one in which everyone was welcome and no superstitious rituals had to be kept secret.

What are we talking about?

It may seem strange to bring up the issue of openness on the heels of secrecy. How can you practise both at the same time? Allow me to explain. While we keep secret the good that we do so that God alone is honoured, we are open about the way God is working in our lives to the same end.

> Openness calls us to abandon secret sin, self-protection and defensiveness.

Openness involves a willingness to embrace truth and the people who bear it. It calls us to abandon secret sin, self-protection and defensiveness. We freely invite God to work in our lives through whatever agents He may choose and we open our hearts to those agents, whether believers, unbelievers, material blessing or physical want.

Biblical background

It interests me that the Apostle Paul felt compelled to write to his friends in Corinth about this. It seems that they had closed their hearts to such a degree that he admonished them: *"Open your hearts to us. We have wronged no one, we have corrupted no one, we have cheated no one. I do not say this to condemn; for I have said before that you are in our hearts, to die together and to live together"* (2 Cor. 7:2-3 NKJV).

"We have spoken freely to you, Corinthians, and opened wide our hearts to you. We are not withholding our affection from you, but you are withholding yours from us. As a fair exchange – I speak as to my children – open wide your hearts also" (2 Cor. 6:11-13 NIV).

In fact, the universe is in a state of openness before God. Our personal openness acknowledges reality as it stands and puts us consciously in the position of being able to receive from Him. *"Nothing in all creation is hidden from God's sight. Everything is uncovered and laid bare before the eyes of him to whom we must give account"* (Heb. 4:13 NIV).

"Do you bring in a lamp to put it under a bowl or a bed? Instead, don't you put it on its stand? For whatever is hidden is meant to be disclosed, and whatever is concealed is meant to be brought out into the open. If anyone has ears to hear, let him hear" (Mark 4:21-23 NIV).

Exploring openness

In a world where people routinely have a negative impact on each other, it is common for us to learn to close down to protect ourselves psychologically. For some this comes tragically early, when as children they suffer at the hands of those who should be most committed to their nurture. For the rest of us, this shutting down comes later, after we've learned how much pain people can inflict on us when we're most vulnerable.

Openness creates the spiritual environment where growth is most likely to take place.

It is quite common for this self-protective tendency to throw up blocks to our spiritual development. That growth typically comes in moments of vulnerability when we drop our guard enough for the Spirit of God to instruct and motivate us. If we habitually lock our hearts shut, we hinder this from happening. This is not to say the Holy Spirit can never penetrate the deep part of us where He does His work, but we can grieve and quench Him with our hardness, slowing our spiritual development.

Since our purpose is to find ways to enhance our spiritual growth, it makes sense to identify hindrances to it and intentionally reverse them. This matter of openness is a clear case where conscious action is necessary. Instead of shutting our heart down to protect ourselves, we choose to open ourselves. This creates the spiritual environment where growth is most likely to take place. God works in open hearts.

The down side of this is that as we open our hearts to God, we inevitably make ourselves vulnerable to people who may intentionally or otherwise cause us pain. Because this pain is so real and immediate it easily dominates the somewhat ethereal benefits of spiritual growth. Our response of shutting down emotionally usually stops, or at least reduces, the pain we're experiencing in a marked way. That feels so good that the negative impact on our spiritual life goes unnoticed.

Openness helps us to...
...*avoid the temptation of trying to look better than we are*
...*benefit from the words and lives of others*
...*share the hard lessons we have learned with others*
...*connect with the body of Christ at the deepest levels*
...*develop our relationship with God unhindered by pretense on our part*

In my experience, God often uses human agents to shape us into the likeness of Jesus. If we are open to receive teaching, counsel, admonition, encouragement, and rebuke from others (and not strictly limited to our Christian brothers and sisters), we will enhance our spiritual life. Indeed, we will be the richer for the role they play in our spiritual development. In opening ourselves to them, we will be opening ourselves to God, Himself.

Potential pitfalls

You've probably already been thinking that there needs to be some balance if we are going to be open in a way that provides the needed benefit without causing harm. I agree. Wisdom must be exercised. We must guard against harming others with our openness. This may come from flaunting our Christian liberty in the presence of weaker believers, thus inducing them to sin. It may harm the reputation of others who we have magnanimously forgiven. Forgiving others is a good thing, but putting their sin on public display is not. Some things are best kept private, because people are easily distracted by personal tidbits and miss the benefit of being close to a heart that is open to God and to them.

The same competitive spirit which drives some Christians to hide their faults and crow about their victories drives others to drag out their spiritual dirty laundry. Sometimes a barely-hidden rivalry becomes evident as Christians share increasingly shocking details of the depths of sin in which they walked before God snatched them from the "miry clay and set their feet upon the rock." All for the glory of God, don't you know (and the amazement of those who have lived sheltered lives). To coin a phrase: "in your openness, do not sin."

A word of encouragement

Christians are often charged with phoniness, because everyone knows that sin constantly challenges even the most morally resolute. To pretend that we are not shamefully sinful in our impulses, if not in our actions, is simply dishonest. How refreshing it has been for me over the years to draw near to some old saint who walked closely enough with God that he was able to encourage me in my spiritual battles by telling me about his own.

> *To pretend that we are not shamefully sinful in our impulses, if not in our actions, is simply dishonest.*

While it's possible to become focussed on the legitimate need to protect ourselves, learning to live openly is worth some pain. You may have noticed that regardless of how hard you try to protect yourself, you are subject to a measure of suffering. The grievous thing is that this pain comes with no up side, no benefit. When we accumulate a few scars because we choose to live openly, we have the satisfaction of knowing blessing along with the pain.

Being open to God will inevitably require us to be open to people. For some of us, the very thought is overwhelming. Fear not! The long-term blessings that come from living with an open heart far exceed the short-term unpleasantness of a bit of criticism, a few harsh words, and some unfair social slighting.

It won't come all at once, but may I encourage you to start heading in the direction of opening your heart to God and to others. Your life will be enriched and you'll soon find that though some will be threatened by your new approach to life, many more will be attracted to it. They will draw near and be blessed as your closer walk with God overflows.

13. Connect with Others

A story to start

We were a family of natural fishermen, my father along with my brother, James, and me. I can't remember a time when we weren't preparing to fish, out on the water casting the nets, or on the beach selling the catch. My life consisted of that simple cycle repeating endlessly. I am John, son of Zebedee.

We socialized exclusively with other fishermen. Had to, really, because we were out of sync with everyone else. We fished all night, sold our catch in the morning, went home to sleep, and just as the sun was setting, got ready to spend another night with the nets out on the water.

That's not to say we were slaves to the trade or obsessive about it. No! We knew how to have fun. Some people thought we were a rather rough lot. Maybe because we were such an exclusive little group always going when everyone else was coming. We'd be getting our work day underway, just as everyone else was trying to settle for the night. Maybe we did make more noise than necessary sometimes, but I think they were just oversensitive.

I was initiated into that group of fishermen before I can remember. James, three years older than me, was always helping dad and, as the little brother, I wasn't about to be outdone. As soon as my mother would let me out of her sight, I was with the men. I don't ever remember being alone. I don't think I'd have known what to do with myself.

I went from being the youngest of that little band of fishermen to being the youngest of the little band of Jesus' disciples. Looking back, I'm rather embarrassed by my own immaturity. I was an instigator, always shaking things up. Sometimes, James would be drawn into whatever craziness I was up to or, more commonly, leap in, big brother style, and save me from myself.

I don't recall what triggered it, but I remember that at some point Jesus started calling James and me the "sons of thunder" because of our brashness. I got rather a kick out of our reputation, though James less so.

In spite of my immaturity at the time, Jesus took me to His heart in a special way. The other disciples didn't seem to mind the closeness of our bond. Perhaps they figured that if I stayed within arm's reach of Jesus, I'd not get into trouble. They were right about that. He had such an influence on me personally that I still shake my head at it.

Maybe He chose me to follow Him because I was so young and would live longer to personally carry His message farther into the next generations. Whatever His motive, I was so blessed by the fellowship we enjoyed together. I learned so much being close to Him and not just from His words, which I never missed. I also learned from His heart, which showed itself in countless ways only one as close as I was could see – a touch, a flicker of a smile, a furrowed brow.

Knowing Jesus was the culmination of my social interactions. From the bosom of my family, to our little band of Galilean fisherman, to the inner circle of Jesus' most trusted disciples, I realize that my whole life had been one of connectedness, closeness, and fellowship.

That's ironic now. I have a terrible memory of my first time alone. I was already a grown man. After the mob arrested Jesus, we all ran for it. Peter and I waited at some little distance then followed them back into the city to the High Priest's house. Because I was known to him and his servants, I was able to get us into the courtyard. I pushed forward to get within earshot of Jesus' accusers; Peter hung back.

When they took the Lord to Pilate, I looked around for Peter to accompany me. He was gone. As I wandered the streets looking for the other disciples, the loneliness was unbearable. Never before had I been without a companion. I felt as if I had been abandoned. I didn't dare imagine what Jesus must have been feeling.

At last, I went to the house where the women were staying. I was so glad to see them! I remained there until word came that

Connect with Others

the crucifixion squad had taken Jesus out of the city. We rushed to the place and watched from a distance. At last, Mary insisted we draw near and Jesus, knowing that we both needed to belong, asked us to take care of each other. We did that until she died.

Now, exiled on an island, I only have memories of fellowship. In some ways that makes it more difficult for me because I know what I've lost. Oh for the joy of simple companionship — a warm smile, a hearty laugh, a common care, a heart-to-heart conversation. Yet, now that I spend so much time alone, I enjoy reflecting on the good times. Lately, the Lord has become very present to me. It's almost like the old days. I've started writing another book. I hope you'll have a chance to read it.

What are we talking about?

Fellowship implies commonality, companionship and community. Fellowship only exists where individuals have a mutual interest. For Christians, the common interest is the Lord Jesus Christ as Saviour and, by extension everything else related to Him – His teaching, His example, His commands, His church and so on.

Fellowship allows us to fulfill the corporate aspects of our faith. There is no biblical precedent for baptism or communion as individual practices. We learn from and gain strength from other believers. I'm sure I would have given up long ago if it were not for the encouragement of other Christians. Tied to this is the fact that each of us is stronger when we are part of a community than we are as individuals. Fellowship provides opportunities to serve Christ as He is embodied in those around us and teaches us to overcome the world's emphasis on individualism.

> *Each of us is stronger when we are part of a community than we are as individuals.*

Fellowship comes in two flavours, universal and local. In a sense, all believers everywhere are in fellowship with each other (regardless of what denominational headquarters may decree), but there is a special sense of connectedness between believers in a particular community because they have the privilege of meeting together, interacting, and working together for the Kingdom.

Biblical background

Several biblical passages underscore the significance of fellowship. Some use the word itself; some use other words in promoting the concept.

"For where two or three come together in my name, there am I with them" (Matt. 18:20 NIV).

"They devoted themselves to the apostles' teaching and to the fellowship, to the breaking of bread and to prayer" (Acts 2:42 NIV).

"If you have any encouragement from being united with Christ, if any comfort from his love, if any fellowship with the Spirit, if any tenderness and compassion, then make my joy complete..." (Phil.2:1-2 NIV).

"But if we walk in the light as He is in the light, we have fellowship with one another, and the blood of Jesus Christ His Son cleanses us from all sin" (1 John 1:7 ESV).

With the exception of specific times when He chose to be alone with His Father, Jesus lived in constant fellowship with His disciples during His time on Earth.

Since His ascension and the coming of the Spirit, each individual believer carries within his or her being the presence of God, but... and this is very important, fellowship allows us to experience the presence of Christ in community—something we can never do on our own.

The love we bear our fellow believers is evidence that we are what we say we are—Christians. Those who find fellowship with Christians unpleasant or unfruitful should heed Paul's words: *"examine yourselves, to see whether you are in the faith"* (2 Cor. 13:5 ESV).

Connect with Others

Exploring fellowship

Our enjoyment of most experiences in life is enhanced when we can share them with someone else. The Bible calls such sharing of experience "fellowship." Fellowship is the other side of the solitude coin. Each balances the other. Each helps us enjoy the other. Each strengthens us to practise the other.

I am amazed (and sometimes amused) by the differences between people in the body of Christ. It seems that in every area of life they live at opposite ends of the spectrum, but their knowledge of and love for the Lord Jesus draws them together to such a degree that they will make significant personal sacrifices for each other and set aside their comfort and preferences to accommodate the other. Jesus told His followers that they could be identified as such by their love for each other. (See John 13:34-35.)

> "The way we are with each other is the truest test of our faith. How I treat a brother or sister from day to day, how I react to the sinscarred wino on the street, how I respond to interruptions from people I dislike, how I deal with normal people in their normal confusion on a normal day may be a better indication of my reverence for life than the anti-abortion sticker on the bumper of my car."[1]

Practically, there are things we can do to increase the benefits of fellowship. We can be intentional about connecting with other Christians in our workplace and community as well as in our church. The Spirit indwells all believers and when two Christians come together on the shop floor, in the office, at school, on the street, or wherever, there is a spiritual resonance that reminds us

> Fellowship should be the other side of the solitude coin. Each balances the other. Each helps us enjoy the other. Each strengthens us to practise the other.

> **Fellowship helps us to...**
> ...experience the presence of Christ in community
> ...fulfill the corporate aspects of our salvation
> ...learn from and gain strength from other believers
> ...be stronger as part of a community than we could ever be as individuals
> ...serve Christ as He is embodied in others
> ...overcome the world's value of hyperindividualism

that we are all part of the body of Christ. Do you sense that?

Because of the tendency of some of us to be wary of people we don't know, fellowship is usually quite superficial at first. To go deeper, you need to become part of a small group. The group needs to be small enough that you can risk being open with other Christians. That's the only way to deepen your fellowship with them. And the deeper your fellowship with others the deeper will be your fellowship with God. Scary thought? Listen to this: *"... he who does not love his brother whom he has seen, how can he love God whom he has not seen?"* (1 John 4:20 NKJV).

Perhaps I haven't mentioned, though you probably noticed, that these *19 ways to boost your spiritual life* are going to stretch you as few things have, or likely ever will.

Potential pitfalls

Of course, some dangers are associated with fellowship. Just as we can be strengthened by our godly brothers and sisters, we can be weakened by the carnal ones—especially when they think they are godly. In his book "Life Together," Dietrich Bonhoeffer wrote about the hazard of "the pious fellowship" which permits no one to be a sinner. In such situations, everyone conceals personal sin from the group. Convinced they are the only sinner in the group, they are horrified when someone else's sin comes into the open and often react in a harsh judgmental way. So, in spite of all the time they spend together, Christians may be terribly alone. In pretending to have overcome sin, they hinder true fellowship.

The adopting of a superficial view of fellowship is a danger. Some always connect food with "fellowship." Others associate finances with the word. They never give money to a needy brother; they "have fellowship" with him. Food and finances are part of fellowship, but we strip the word of its significance if we exclude appropriate spiritual intimacy from its meaning.

Lastly, there is the danger of becoming isolated in a small group instead of using our fellowship times to prepare us to reach out to unbelievers and to other Christians in the broader community. The fellowship of a small group should not become a substitute for our being consciously and effectively part of a whole local church as it comes together. Fellowship can become so precious to us that it upsets the balanced life to which God calls us.

A word of encouragement

Fellowship is one of those things that is so wonderful that it can become an end in itself. "Let the good times roll." All Christians know the joy of being connected with like-minded believers for encouragement and edification. We get our social needs met as well as spiritual ones, so it's easy for our focus to shift to that which is more immediate, more tangible, and more instantly accessible.

The kind of relationship described as "iron sharpening iron" has, as the metaphor suggests, an edge to it. The good news is that the closer we walk with Christ, the less likely we are to see our Christian fellowship degenerate into just another

> *The kind of relationship described as "iron sharpening iron" has, as the metaphor suggests, an edge to it.*

party. One of the ways that we learn to walk more closely with Christ is by walking more closely and transparently with our brothers and sisters. The good news is that what could, if we were careless, deteriorate and lose its value, can, if we are careful, improve and become ever more valuable.

---

1. Manning, Brennan—www.supercinski.net/2008/06/29/quotes-on-fellowship/

14. Learn to Submit

A story to start

Never question if deep inner change is possible. It is not easy. It is not quick. But it does happen. It happened to me. I am Peter, fisherman and fisher of men.

In childhood I developed my tendency to say the first thought that came into my head – to state it before others had a chance to state their thoughts – and to begin action immediately, before anyone else could get his plan under way. By the time I was a man, it seemed this was the only way I could function.

I tried to learn. I tried to change. I embarrassed myself so many times. I blurted out things I regretted. But spoken words are like water poured on the ground. I'm still haunted by a few spectacular attempts to be the first one off the mark but the last one to get to the finish line.

I told the Lord His prediction that He would die on the cross would not happen. I didn't intend to let it happen and He identified me with Satan. On the mountain, I suggested we make shrines for Jesus, Moses and Elijah and the very voice of God said, "This is the Son I love. Listen to Him." I leapt in with my sword, ready to be a hero, to defend my Lord, and He told me to put it away and healed the man I'd hurt. I told Jesus I would die before I would betray Him and my own words condemned me as I denied Him three times before sunup the next day.

I felt condemned to be known so widely for my impetuosity. Then something happened. At Pentecost the Spirit of God came. A new dimension entered my life – new power, but just as significantly, new restraint. I had never understood how the Lord could submit himself to the hands of His torturers and executioners. And suddenly, I knew. I didn't figure it out. No one taught me. I just... knew.

And my life changed. I changed. I didn't have to be in control anymore. When John and I were arrested and taken before the council, I didn't resist. I spoke the truth boldly, but with respect for the men to whom I spoke. God was showing me things and I was responding. A Roman sent for me and I not only went to his house, I went inside! I spoke the word of the Lord to him and his family and witnessed God come into their lives.

On another occasion I was arrested and put into prison. I went quietly and just as quietly I followed an angel past two ranks of guards and out of that prison, though to tell the truth that was a little unsettling. But I was learning that God was in control and if I submitted to Him, submitting to humans was no challenge. He would take care of everything. If I acknowledged that He was in charge and didn't try to fix things myself, He'd fix things.

Later, there was trouble in the church. We held a council in Jerusalem. Emotions ran high. Tempers flared. We all had a sense that we were contending for the truth of God. By God's grace I was able to stand and deliver a short testimony of my own which resulted in a spirit of calm settling over the crowd. Usually, when I spoke I stirred things up, but when I submitted to the Holy Spirit and kept my passions under control, good things happened.

Then there was the incident in Antioch. I knew then that God had really changed me. Under the influence of some strict Jews who visited from Jerusalem, I had foolishly reverted to some of my traditional Jewish ways. Paul tackled me on it – and not quietly in private. Right there in a public meeting! In front of the whole congregation, Paul held me accountable for my behaviour. He challenged me to my face and went on to teach about freedom from the law. I didn't enjoy it, but I knew he was right. My submission to God had made it possible for me to submit to my brother.

I know there is more submission ahead of me. Jesus Himself prophesied that I had one ultimate act of submission to endure. At the time He said it, I rebelled inwardly. Now, I'm content to let it happen. I will go His way. Gladly.

What are we talking about?

Simply put, submission is the surrender of power or authority to another. It involves voluntarily deferring to someone else's will, opinion, judgment or desire.

Biblical background

Because the concept is counter-cultural, it's important to establish the biblical background, especially noting that **all** Christians are called to submit to others. Specifically, we are to submit to:

God *"Submit yourselves therefore to God. Resist the devil, and he will flee from you. Draw near to God, and he will draw near to you. Cleanse your hands, you sinners, and purify your hearts, you double-minded. Be wretched and mourn and weep. Let your laughter be turned to mourning and your joy to gloom. Humble yourselves before the Lord, and he will exalt you"* (Jas. 4:7-10 ESV).

Civil Authority *"Be subject for the Lord's sake to every human institution, whether it be to the emperor as supreme, or to governors as sent by him to punish those who do evil and to praise those who do good. For this is the will of God, that by doing good you should put to silence the ignorance of foolish people"* (1 Pet. 2:13-15 ESV).

Church Authority *"Obey your leaders and submit to them, for they are keeping watch over your souls, as those who will have to give an account. Let them do this with joy and not with groaning..."* (Hebrews 13:17 ESV).

Each other *"Submit to one another out of reverence for Christ"* (Eph. 5:21 NIV). *"Yes, all of you be submissive to one another, and be clothed with humility, for 'God resists the proud, But gives grace to the humble'"* (1 Pet. 5:5 NKJV). *"Do nothing from rivalry or conceit, but in humility count others more significant than yourselves. Let each of you look not only to his own interests, but also to the interests of others"* (Phil. 2:3-4 ESV).

Exploring submission

This is one of the most challenging areas of spiritual life to discuss because it goes against the grain of human personality. It is not considered a virtue in western culture. As well, even within the Christian context, nearly everyone has some negative baggage associated with submission.

- Some feel they have tried submission and "it didn't work."
- Some see submission as a cultural artifact that has no place in contemporary society.
- Some feel they have the right to demand submission from certain others in their lives.
- Most of us have experienced abuse, legitimized as someone's "right" to our submission.
- Nearly everyone focusses on the energy flow from the "submitter" to the "submittee" and entirely misses the flow in the other direction. Those in leadership are to use their authority for the benefit of their followers.

While submission is not valued and not discussed much in the broader culture, it is valued and does show up as a relatively common theme in the Bible. But the biblical concept of submission is more about the appropriate attitude than about hierarchy. It emphasizes submission's voluntary nature over coerced subjugation and teaches mutuality among Christians, calling us to value, respect, and honour our fellow believers. Biblical submission will always make us more like Jesus.

Throughout the Gospels, we constantly see Jesus in submission to the Father. Sometimes He underscores this with His words, as in: *"When you have lifted up the Son of Man, then you will know that I am he, and that I do nothing on my own authority, but speak just as the Father taught me. And he who sent me is with me. He has not left me alone, for I always do the things that are pleasing to him"* (John 8:28-29 ESV). But even when He wasn't verbalizing it, He lived it out. We find the most striking example in that mysterious moment in the Garden of Gethsemane when, stretching everything we know about the unity of the godhead, Jesus prayed, *"Father, if you are willing, take this cup from me; yet not my will, but yours be done"* (Luke 22:42 NIV).

In Jesus' words we see the difference between submission and obedience. One can perform the outward acts of obedience without the inner attitude of submission. However, the inner attitude of submission always leads to the outward acts of obedience. This is what we find in the Lord Jesus and this is what others should find in us.

Submission helps us to...
...learn how to surrender control
...learn to recognize legitimate authority and how to function under it
...learn how to receive criticism (legitimate and illegitimate)
...learn how to be accountable
...develop a soft heart and a teachable spirit
...accept that we are ultimately under Christ
...receive spiritual guidance and wisdom
...free ourselves from the bondage of being in control
...free ourselves from self-exaltation

To get started practising submission, invite trusted people to point out your spiritual weaknesses. This can be of great benefit especially if you invite them to hold you accountable. Then, monitor your reaction when anyone points out flaws, faults, weaknesses, or sin. If you can embrace their input, you're on the right track. If you get defensive, you have some spiritual work ahead.

Those who practise submission effectively, often find themselves moving into places of spiritual leadership. If you look at the men and women God used as leaders, you'll find they learned to be followers first.

Potential pitfalls

It was hard to decide whether these potential pitfalls should be addressed to the "submitters" or the "submittees." Appropriate admonitions to one group have their corollaries appropriate for the other. Here, I've opted to speak to those who are called to submit. Those to whom that submission is due should make the appropriate application.

Problems in this area are mostly associated with a distorted view of submission. We need to be careful to avoid letting someone else take the place of God in our life. We do need to submit to others, but we must never give them inappropriate control. Because we live in a fallen world, sometimes acts of civil disobedience are called for as we submit to God. Human authorities, whether in the home, social institutions, or even the church must sometimes be disobeyed by godly Christians when that authority attempts to force them to behave in ways that are clearly against God.

Even in cases where there is no overt attempt to lead us away from God, some to whom we are called to submit may attempt to dominate us to such a degree that we lose our sense of identity and unique value. This can hinder us from fulfilling our responsibilities before God. God has made us as He has for His purposes, not for us to be consumed or dominated by others.

Finally, be sure you don't try to manipulate others through submission. We can easily fall into some form of psychological deal making thinking, *If I submit to you, you owe me.*

A word of encouragement

Living in the 21st Century, you're going to need all the help you can get. You will get no support, let alone encouragement from the culture around you. Today's cultural icons consistently flout the rules, challenge authority, reject social norms, and despise biblical standards. This is not to say that you will find no encouragement from individuals who do not have a relationship with Jesus. Wonderful people from all kinds of philosophical background may spur you on in a variety of ways. That said, the culture, in general, tends away from God and godliness.

> *"Submit to God. Resist the devil and he will flee from you" (James 4:7 NKJV).*

The most encouraging thing I can say is what James already said in chapter four of his letter. There he notes that submission is the first step to spiritual victory. Want to defeat Satan? Don't start by trying to bind him, or cast him out, or otherwise do battle with him. Start by submitting to God. Then resist him through the Word in the power of the Spirit and he will flee from you. Jesus won the most intense spiritual battle in the cosmos by submitting, to God first, then to all of the other authorities—religious, civil, judicial—that the Father would use to accomplish His purposes.

Nobody will tell you that submission is fun, that it's a real ego-booster, that it'll make you look good or make you rich. Submission is a trial for all of us, particularly if we see it as giving in to the people God wants to use as agents of change in our lives and not as to God, Himself. Only those who learn to submit to God and His often unfathomable ways will know the supreme joy of real spiritual victory.

15. Study Your Bible

A story to start

When the voice of God is no longer heard through the prophets, the only source of truth is the Scriptures. That is what Pharisees give their lives to discovering. I know this because I am a Pharisee. I search for truth in the Torah. My name is Nicodemus.

Study. That is the story of my life in one word. From the time I learned to read I have been fascinated with words. Words are the smallest building blocks of communication and in the Torah we have the words of God. If we want to know what God is saying to us, we must explore every syllable. But that is not enough.

Undue emphasis on words by themselves can lead to grave error. We must also make connections—all the connections. God never contradicts Himself, so we challenge every seeming incongruity. We connect all of the related thoughts. We assemble all of the little pieces as parts of one gigantic whole.

One would think that after all these years of study, we'd be approaching the end—at least getting close to having all the loose ends tied together nicely and having one final clear concept of God and His law. One would think that, but it is not the case. I'm not a young man anymore. I've been doing this for more than thirty years. The last while, I've felt further from the truth than ever.

The last prophet who spoke the word of the Lord to His people was Malachi – that was 400 years ago. All we have now is the Scriptures. So we study. One rabbi will express an opinion. Another will offer an alternative view. We debate the issue in the council. Some days these sessions seem interminable. We never seem to be getting any closer to the truth. There is no authoritative guiding voice. At least there hasn't been.

Now suddenly, a man shows up. He's an itinerant rabbi (without credentials, I might add) from Galilee, teaching in the temple courts. Here's the dilemma. We Pharisees have given our lives to studying the Torah. While I've admitted we don't have everything sorted out, we have been able to be definitive about a lot of things. But this man, is disturbing everything.

He teaches that God is not interested in the careful outward observance of the law, though this is the one conclusion on which all of the previous rabbis agree. Instead of teaching the many individual laws which are well defined and measurable, He reduces the whole 613 specific laws to two general ones. Firstly, love God with heart, soul, strength and mind and, secondly, love your neighbour as yourself. How do you measure that? No one would be able to claim to have kept those laws—not even my colleagues in the council and I.

Two things are thorns in our flesh. First is His popularity. He barely opens His mouth and crowds throng Him. We can barely get our own students to listen to us. Second is that indefinable "something" about Him. Though He seems to break many of the laws, there is no doubt He is a holy man. He knows God in a way I don't. He speaks for God in a way that no rabbi of my acquaintance has.

Late last night, I visited Him. As I approached Him, I got the impression that He had been waiting for me. He answered all of my questions. His responses were both clear and puzzling. He spoke of birth as a spiritual thing. To be a child of God means being born of God—born from above. I challenged Him. A mature man can't be born a second time. But how else could one get new life—eternal life? I must spend more time studying this.

What are we talking about?

Along with prayer, Bible study tops most people's experience with things they do intentionally to help themselves to grow spiritually. Perhaps we should dare to ask ourselves if what we do is really "study" or if we stop somewhat short of making the effort implied by the word. Study involves the exercise of our intellectual powers to acquire knowledge, understanding and wisdom—typically through reading or experimentation. It suggests deep thought about the subject and requires mental processing of the data as opposed to merely recording facts in our memory. For the committed, there are various approaches to disciplined Bible study. These methods are the subjects of entire books and seminary courses. As you progress, you may want to dig into some of these.

Biblical background

Among several biblical references to study is Jesus' words to the Pharisees in John 5: *"You search the Scriptures because you think that in them you have eternal life; and it is they that bear witness about me, yet you refuse to come to me that you may have life"* (John 5:39-40 ESV). The Scriptures pointed to Jesus as the Messiah, but the Pharisees did not respond.

Study was an activity of the early church: *"Now these Jews [the ones in Berea] were more noble than those in Thessalonica; they received the word with all eagerness, examining the Scriptures daily to see if these things were so"* (Acts 17:11 ESV).

Paul had several things to say about study. He challenged Timothy: *"Do your best to present yourself to God as one approved, a worker who has no need to be ashamed, rightly handling the word of truth"* (2 Tim. 2:15 ESV) and wrote to the Romans: *"... whatever was written in former days was written for our instruction, that through endurance and through the encouragement of the Scriptures we might have hope"* (Rom. 15:4 ESV).

Exploring study

Study helps us to align our understanding of reality with God's. The Bible sometimes seems inscrutable, but this impression is lessened if we diligently apply the best methods of study to clarifying our understanding. Study is necessary to discover God's truth revealed in the Bible. Some of it can be discerned in little more than a cursory reading. Some must be mined with considerable mental effort. But "study" applied to God's word does not stop with the mere apprehension of the facts.

Its purpose is to conform our minds and thinking to God's. Transformation and renewal are good words to describe what we hope to gain from Bible study.

Study helps us to...
...align our understanding of reality with God's.
...discover God's truth revealed in the Bible (facts, reality, truth).
...conform our minds and thinking to align with God's.
...know God.

As with all of these *19 ways to boost our spiritual life*, we need to be intentional about Bible study. Regardless of its frequency, Bible study time must be purposefully chosen. While we may pick up the Bible to read on a casual basis, we need to be more deliberate about setting aside time for study.

It seems to go without saying, but we need to pay attention when we study. One of the reasons we forget so easily is that we don't truly pay attention. It helps to eliminate distractions as much as possible — this includes distractions both in your environment and in your mind. And be firm with yourself. When your attention drifts, consciously pull it back. Making notes will help you know where to come back to when you wander. Most of us have to be both intentional and determined.

One of the real values of study comes with making connections. Connect new material with what you already know. These connections help us assemble the truth of the Bible into a "big picture" view which leads to an understanding of the whole. Connections also help us to filter out erroneous ideas because they won't fit with the big picture.

For most of us repetition is valuable in locking information in our memory. There are several approaches to memorization. Some prefer to learn individual verses, others concentrate on memorizing chapter themes within a book. Still others champion the value of learning the links which tie specific ideas to the big picture.

There is one more thing I'll mention here, though we've already considered it on its own. That is meditation. As we go over nuggets of truth repeatedly, we'll deepen our understanding and achieve our goals in studying.

Potential pitfalls

The most dangerous pitfall associated with this lofty practice may lie in the realm of motives. We need to guard against the desire to arm ourselves to demolish others who see things differently. Study for this purpose will taint the results and nullify the potential spiritual benefit associated with it. We also need to guard against being satisfied with an academic mastery of the text. While understanding the Bible's concepts at the level of words, phrases and sentences, if we stop short of allowing the Truth to make a positive impact in our lives, we've shortchanged ourselves.

Another very real danger is doing all of your study on your own. Much and all as we might like to think we'll always get it right when we try to submit to the Spirit as we study the Bible, we can get it wrong. Discuss what you are learning with wise mature Christians and compare your insights with those of others who have gone before.

A word of encouragement

Study of the Bible can enrich our spiritual lives in ways that nothing else can. It not only challenges our intellect and stimulates our emotions, it deepens our relationship with the Author. As you embark on ever more serious seasons of study, remember that its purpose is not to allow us to conquer the material, but to allow God to conquer our hard hearts and shape us into the likeness of Jesus.

16. Worship

A story to start

Seven years is a long time to wait for something you want very much. Yet the moment it is realized, the wait seems to have been nothing. I am Solomon, Son of David, King of Israel.

In honour of my father's dream to build a dwelling place for God on earth, I have built the most magnificent temple imaginable. It was a task entrusted to me and I have been zealous not merely to carry it out as a obligation, but to exceed all expectations so that the building itself is a monument of worship to the Maker and Lord of the universe.

This temple is the place where all peoples will come to worship the Most High. Here they will raise their hands in prayer. Here they will prostrate themselves before Him. Here they will slay the animals which atone for their sins. Here they will celebrate the goodness and mercy of the God who has redeemed His people from bondage. Here they will experience intimacy with Jehovah, Himself, as He comes to dwell in the midst of the praises of His people.

Such a place must be worthy of its purpose. It must be large for God is awesome. It must be magnificent for God is glorious. It must be held sacred for God is holy.

More than seven years have passed since work on the foundation was begun. Day by day it took shape before my eyes. When the construction was finished, I came and saw the work of our hands. It was spectacular, yet it was nothing more than a great quiet empty space. It was a lonely place devoid of the presence of workmen, of worshippers, of priests, of God.

We filled it with furnishings and the treasures my father had dedicated to it. It was now the most valuable acre on the face of the earth—magnificent in design, exquisite in execution, lavish in its accoutrements. I explored its halls and chambers and was filled with a sense of emptiness.

Yesterday, we came together to bring the ark of the covenant, from its temporary home prepared by my father, to its permanent dwelling place behind the veil of the temple in the most holy place. As we made the journey, we sacrificed countless sheep and oxen—the best of the land—as an act of worship.

Finally we carried it through the successive temple courts until, at last, the ark rested between the cherubim in the most holy place. Only the tips of the poles on which it had been carried were visible and only from the holy place. Only the priests whose lot it was to serve that day stayed there. The rest of us retired to the courtyard.

The priests and Levites gathered at the east end of the altar. They were all dressed in fine white linen and carried instruments (there were 120 priests with trumpets alone). As one, the singers and musicians lifted up their praise. It was as if the whole nation had but one great voice praising the Lord.

As they were saying the words "For the Lord is good, for His mercy endures forever," a great shining cloud filled the whole structure. The glory of the Lord filled the house of God. The priests who had remained in the holy place came reeling out. Barely able to stand, they sought refuge from the overwhelming presence with us in the temple courtyard.

Truly, words fail me. The sun shining on the white marble and gold, the sound of the musicians crying out songs of adoration, and the palpable presence of God filling the temple left our hearts at once broken, bursting, and overflowing.

I prayed on behalf of my people, magnifying our God and pledging our faithfulness and when I finished, fire. A flash of pure white light split the sky and consumed the burnt offering and sacrifices. The glory of God was so real, so alive, so concrete the priests could not enter. We fell with our faces to the ground and sang those words that brought His glory down, "The Lord is good, for His mercy endures forever."

Whatever else we knew at the end of that day, we knew we had been in the presence of God. We knew that we had worshipped.

What are we talking about?

As I looked at definitions of worship, I observed that some had rather mechanical aspects—bowing, crouching, prostrating, for example. In true worship, these are merely physical postures reflecting a condition of the heart which is difficult to express. What matters more than the outward expressions is the inward condition. Worship is our appropriate response to God as Omnipotent Creator, King of the Universe, and personal Lord and Saviour. Several associated words help us fill out the concept: respect, honour, reverence, adoration, adulation, devotion, love.

"When I worship, I would rather my heart be without words than my words be without heart..."[1]

Biblical background

We often associate the Psalms with worship. We certainly find expressions of worship there, but much more common is the call to worship. For example: *"Exalt the LORD our God, And worship at His footstool—He is holy... Exalt the LORD our God, And worship at His holy hill; For the LORD our God is holy"* (Psalm 99:5,9 NKJV). The psalmists repeatedly encourage worship through their poetry. They recount the greatness of God and His works, His faithfulness, His provision and so on, with the desire that those who are exposed to the psalms would be stimulated to respond appropriately to God.

Moving to the New Testament, we find Jesus quoting the Old Testament to Satan. In response to his temptation, Jesus said to him, *"Away with you, Satan! For it is written, 'You shall worship the LORD your God, and Him only you shall serve'"* (Matt. 4:10 NKJV). John's Gospel emphasizes the inner aspect of worship in recording the words of Jesus: *"God is Spirit, and those who worship Him must worship in spirit and truth"* (John 4:24 NKJV). In the light of these words, physical postures, ritual prayers, and religious traditions are pushed back to give priority to our attitude toward God.

Exploring worship

Worship helps us to...
...engage our entire being (heart, soul, mind and strength) with God
...fulfill the explicit command of God
...respond appropriately to One who made us for His pleasure

The first biblical reference to worship occurs in Genesis 22 when Abraham tells his servants to stay with the donkey while he and Isaac proceed a little farther to worship. Abraham's willingness to part with the dearest thing in his life—his son, heir and fulfilment of God's promise—sets a high standard as we begin to think about worship in our own lives.

I tend to keep using the expression "true worship." I shouldn't have to, but I know from my own experience that it is all too easy to go through the forms of worship with an entirely inappropriate attitude toward God. Human observers would be easily deceived. Indeed! I believe I often deceive myself, but God knows whether or not I am worshipping at all. True worship, as opposed to that which superficially passes for worship, engages our entire being (heart, soul, mind, and strength) with God. It has both private and corporate, inner and outer aspects which we need to keep in balance.

Several biblical writers expressed commands to worship in one way or another. I believe this is mostly necessary because so often the people of God do not experience His presence in a vital way, perhaps not in any way at all. I say this, because in every instance in Scripture where people encountered God in person, they worshipped. No one had to tell them to do it. It was the spontaneous response of the human heart to its Maker.

One thing that many have found useful is the development of the art of practising the presence of God—recognizing God moment by moment in the occurrences of the day. Make an effort to prepare yourself spiritually before meeting for corporate worship (read and reflect on a Bible passage, meditate on the words of a hymn, arrive early and quieten your mind and heart.)

> "We only learn to behave ourselves in the presence of God."[2]

In corporate prayer, seek a sense of community with an awareness that you are individuals who have come together before God. Be aware of the worship of others around you as well as what is happening in your own spirit. Develop worship in your life as a regular practice, not just something you do at the emotional level when you feel like it. Speak words of worship even in your distress and pain. Reach for God physically with your hands as well as figuratively with your heart.

Potential pitfalls

I can think of no danger in worship itself, no way to overdo it, but harm can come from distortions. We often confuse worship with our preferred form of worship. We err when we enshrine our mode of worship as definitive. Not only do we find ourselves condemning our Christian brothers and sisters needlessly, but we also block ourselves in and limit our expression to what we've been comfortable with in the past.

Another distortion that can present problems is attempting to please ourselves with worship rather than focussing on God. We don't worship to be

> "Just as worship begins in holy expectancy, it ends in holy obedience. Holy obedience saves worship from becoming an opiate, an escape from the pressing needs of modern life."[3]

blessed, though often we are blessed when we worship. The motive must relate to our honouring God, not giving ourselves a "positive worship experience."

We can also lose balance between worship as a subjective individual experience and as an objective corporate activity. Retreating into our own inner space, even when we are in a public worship setting is as much a problem as convincing ourselves that we can only worship in large groups, preferably with a decent band, appropriate lighting and perhaps other amenities.

A word of encouragement

To enrich your worship, study biblical passages dealing with the subject, especially noting the things you find would expand your usual form of worship. Experiment with alternative expressions of worship (large group, small group, private). If you usually worship liturgically, try being spontaneous in your expression. If you are usually spontaneous, try writing down your expressions of worship and make use of liturgical resources. Try engaging all aspects of your being in worship—intellect, emotions, will, body, and spirit.

> "Worship is first and foremost for His benefit, not ours, though it is marvellous to discover that in giving Him pleasure, we ourselves enter into what can become our richest and most wholesome experience in life."[4]

---

1. Boschman, LaMar—http://www.goodreads.com/quotes/show/120856
2. Lewis, C. S.—http://209.237.184.2/prayer/ Devotional_50DaysWithGod_3.asp
3. Foster, Richard—http://dailychristianquote.com/dcqfosterrj.html
4. Kendrick, Graham—http://www.theocentricworship.com/

17. Embrace Suffering

A story to start

Some things a man doesn't choose. I'd be the first to argue that we do have choices. Choices on which all of our future life depends. Choices on which our eternal portion depends! But some things choose the man rather than the other way round. I know this from experience. I am Paul originally from Tarsus, then from Jerusalem, and now I don't even have a place I'd identify as home anymore.

No one would choose a life of suffering. Pain is no end in itself. Yet, one might gladly choose a life which includes a heavy measure of suffering, with the proviso that the end justifies the pain along the way. I would argue that everyone knows tribulation. We are all afflicted by sin—the righteous and the rebellious, the pure and the promiscuous, the wise and the foolish, the serious and the silly. No one is free of suffering so why not choose a life in which the suffering serves some purpose, is not merely the consequence of foolish ideas and trivial motivations, but serves some real benefit in conquering the flesh, shaping the soul and refining the spirit?

Some say I speak as a fool when I say things like this. Am I a fool because my suffering has meaning, or because it is necessary for the blessing of others, or because it makes me more like my Lord? Count me as a fool if you like. If you do, you count the very Christ a fool as well. His suffering had meaning, was necessary for our blessing and made Him the only example worth following.

Perhaps you doubt that I know whereof I speak. Maybe you are ignorant of the world we live in—a world which is hostile to the Christ and His followers. He called me to share His life. His was a life of suffering, so mine must be one of suffering. As I share this calling with the One who called me, I look forward to sharing the glory which must follow. God is just. No suffering goes unnoticed. No suffering is wasted. No suffering goes unrewarded. I may sound like a fool, but wisdom is in my words.

I have been in the company of many men. They have told me their tales. They have boasted of their exploits and victories. I have nothing to tell but my weakness, my shame, my pain and the One who called me to this life and to the glory to come.

I don't tell you this for my benefit. Listen and learn. I work hard, continuously. For that diligence I have been whipped and imprisoned, not once, but many times. I have been close to death. I know what it is to look into heaven itself, to see its unspeakable wonders and be sent back to suffer.

No danger is too much for one who claims the Christ as his Lord. I've suffered three shipwrecks; on one occasion spending a full twenty-four hours in the wintry waters of the Mediterranean Sea. I thought I'd never be warm again.

I've worn out so many sandals, I've lost count. My travels have blistered my feet and stripped the flesh from my body. Follow me for a year and you'll not laugh when I say I no longer know where I am from.

I live with the awareness of danger. I never travel alone. My Jewish countrymen would kill me if they had the chance. The Romans would kill me if they could. Even some who claim to follow the Christ would like to do the world a favour by ridding it of me. The very beasts that share the wilderness with me on my travels would strengthen themselves with my stringy flesh.

Pardon me if this sounds like more foolishness. More boasting. More empty words from a man charged with being a windbag. I'm not telling you the half. I would not try your patience with tales of dungeon songs and stoning on the road. I speak only the truth. The God and Father of our Lord Jesus Christ, who is blessed forever, knows that I am not lying.

While I breathe I lay down my life daily for the sake of the gospel. This pain of mine is digging a deep well from which to draw consolation for my suffering brothers and sisters. Yes, I suffer, but they suffer, too. Yes, I suffer, but He suffered more.

What are we talking about?

In contrast to the anticipated future perfections of heaven, we live currently in a world racked by physical and emotional pain. As I was writing this section, a lady from a Central American country came into the office and poured out story after story of gang violence in her beloved homeland. Extortion, kidnapping, rackets of any and all kinds are part of life in the big cities. No one is safe. Fear is a way of life. In other parts of the world, natural disasters, disease, and famine stalk the most vulnerable. Regardless of what we might see as the root cause of all this, the result is human suffering at a pitch we haven't witnessed before.

Simply put, I'm using "suffering" as a kind of catchall word which includes everything alluded to by more specific words like: tribulation, affliction, distress, hurt, harm, pain and anguish. We'll include any negative or distressing sensation or emotion, whatever its cause. (Some of us inflict a good deal of suffering on ourselves.)

The Bible indicates there are two kinds of suffering. The first is that which is simply the result of being human and living in a sin-contaminated environment. Everyone suffers: the "good," the "bad," the guilty, the innocent, the rich, the poor, the religious, the irreligious. But for Christians, there is an additional suffering. (Doesn't that idea warm your heart?)

God's people in this age are called to suffer for their faith. When some of his women followers tried to comfort Jesus on the way to the cross, He gave a rather ominous reply, some of which I'll quote here: *"Daughters of Jerusalem, do not weep for me, but weep for yourselves and for your children... For if they do these things when the wood is green, what will happen when it is dry?"* (Luke 23:28-31 ESV). Thus the idea of suffering is of particular interest to Christians.

Biblical background

You may notice that the biblical background section is longer for this topic than it is for any other. In part, that is because the

Bible has a lot to say about suffering (and these are just a few notable passages). Also unbiblical teachings out there suggest that God does not intend for His children to suffer and, taken to the extreme, that suffering is sinful. Hopefully these verses will help clear up some of this confusion.

Let's consider what the Bible has to say about this difficult and rather unpopular subject.

- Suffering in this life is promised to believers—*"These things I have spoken to you, that in Me you may have peace. In the world you will have tribulation; but be of good cheer, I have overcome the world"* (John 16:33 NKJV).
- Suffering in this life is a common experience— *"Resist him [the devil], steadfast in the faith, knowing that the same sufferings are experienced by your brotherhood in the world"* (1 Pet. 5:9 NKJV).
- God uses suffering as a means of refining our faith— *"In this you greatly rejoice, though now for a little while, if need be, you have been grieved by various trials, that the genuineness of your faith, being much more precious than gold that perishes, though it is tested by fire, may be found to praise, honour, and glory at the revelation of Jesus Christ"* (1 Pet. 1:6-7 NKJV).
- Great people of God in the past suffered patiently and serve as an example for us—*"My brethren, take the prophets, who spoke in the name of the Lord, as an example of suffering and patience"* (Jas. 5:10 NKJV).
- Christians can help others because of their own experience with suffering—*"Now if we are afflicted, it is for your consolation and salvation, which is effective for enduring the same sufferings which we also suffer. Or if we are comforted, it is for your consolation and salvation"* (2 Cor. 1:6 NKJV).
- Suffering is balanced by consolation if not in this life, in the next—*"And our hope for you is steadfast, because we know that as you are partakers of the sufferings, so also*

Embrace Suffering

you will partake of the consolation" (2 Cor. 1:7 NKJV).

- Suffering is a way of knowing Jesus—*"... that I may know Him and the power of His resurrection, and the fellowship of His sufferings, being conformed to His death"* (Phil. 3:10 NKJV).

- Present suffering is trivial compared to future glory—*"For I consider that the sufferings of this present time are not worthy to be compared with the glory which shall be revealed in us"* (Rom. 8:18 NKJV).

- Suffering develops and matures us, just as it "perfected" Jesus—*"For it was fitting for Him, for whom are all things and by whom are all things, in bringing many sons to glory, to make the captain of their salvation perfect through sufferings"* (Heb. 2:10 NKJV).

In light of all of the above, you might be tempted to think that serious Christians seeking a closer walk with God should be out there looking for suffering and if no one else will hurt them, a little self-flagellation wouldn't be amiss. Of course, if you did think that, you'd be wrong. God is not a sadist and He doesn't require us to be masochists to have a deep relationship with him.

Much of Jesus' earthly ministry involved the alleviation of suffering, so we will attempt to do the same for others and for ourselves as well—*"Is anyone among you suffering? Let him pray. Is anyone cheerful? Let him sing praise. Is anyone among you sick? Let him call for the elders of the church, and let them pray over him, anointing him with oil in the name of the Lord. And the prayer of faith will save the one who is sick, and the Lord will raise him up. And if he has committed sins, he will be forgiven"* (Jas. 5:13 ESV).

Exploring suffering

Let's get one thing onto the table from the start. Suffering is always the consequence of sin. God takes no delight in our suffering. He did not intend for us to even know what it is, but just as surely as I bear the genetic stamp of my forebears back

> **Suffering helps us to...**
> ...understand the seriousness of sin by experiencing its consequences
> ...be able to identify with and comfort others who suffer
> ...experience God's grace in ways we otherwise wouldn't
> ...be conformed to the likeness of Jesus

to the beginning of creation, I also carry their spiritual legacy of rebellion against God. Between my own sinfulness and that of those around me there is no escape from the suffering.

Sometimes in His grace, God intervenes to limit our suffering. At other times, He lets the full impact of sin, be it our own or that of others, to do cleansing redemptive work in our lives. While we may experience something less than maximum suffering, we can't really expect less. We've already considered many verses which accept that suffering will be part of the human experience regardless of our personal philosophy, religious beliefs, physical strength or any other factor we might hope would make a difference.

Let's expand for a moment on the idea that though suffering is inevitable, to be expected and can even have some beneficial effects, it should be alleviated whenever possible to the greatest degree we can. These words from Galatians 6 are particularly applicable: *"Brothers, if anyone is caught in any transgression, you who are spiritual should restore him in a spirit of gentleness. Keep watch on yourself, lest you too be tempted. Bear one another's burdens, and so fulfill the law of Christ"* (Galatians 6:1-2 ESV). Since we are all subject to the effects of sin in our lives, Paul calls us to do what we can to diminish its negative effects in the lives of our brothers and sisters in Christ.

How easy it is for us to unthinkingly (at least I hope it's unthinkingly) add to the suffering of others in the Body of Christ by subjecting them to unkind, unhelpful comments about their various predicaments. We might hide behind the adage "if you can't say something nice, don't say anything," but God does not call us to such a low standard. He invites us to

Embrace Suffering

be like Himself, to take the initiative, to be proactive, to reach out with words and deeds of comfort for the afflicted.

I freely admit that we often feel awkward and helpless in the face of others' pain. Perhaps of help is an observation I made in a time of our own family crisis. I was intrigued by which friends drew near and which ones withdrew. Some approached us confessing their fear of saying something clumsily that might add to our distress, but they came alongside. Others took the easy way out and stayed away. I don't condemn these dear ones. I have been in their shoes too many times to criticize. It wasn't until I experienced the loneliness that often comes with suffering that I saw how important it is to move toward those who are in pain of one kind or another. Those who have suffered are in the best position to console the suffering, but that doesn't let the rest of us off the hook.

> *It wasn't until I experienced the loneliness that often comes with suffering to see how important it is to move toward those who are in pain of one kind or another.*

Lastly in this section, I would be remiss if I didn't remind you that God can redeem our most distressing situations to bless us and glorify Himself. No suffering is pleasant. (If it were, I suspect we wouldn't call it "suffering.") Indeed, it is grievous. Yet, we can miss out on some of the good God intends for us if we insist on feeling sorry for ourselves and refusing to allow Him to use our pain to soften and shape us. We won't always be able to recognize what's happening, but if we keep our hearts soft toward God even as we experience pain, we'll benefit in ways we can't even imagine.

> *God can redeem our most distressing situations to bless us and glorify Himself.*

Potential pitfalls

I can quickly think of two major pitfalls associated with embracing suffering and dealing with it in a godly proactive way. One is that we may be disappointed to learn that we can't fix everything. Our faith may even be shaken. After all, we're just trying to be obedient. We're bearing burdens, learning lessons, trying to glorify God and nothing makes sense.

This leads directly to the other pitfall, that of trying to associate significance or meaning to every instance of pain. Our ways are not God's ways. Our way of thinking is not the same as His. Our perspective is largely limited to our material/temporal existence. He sees the end from the beginning. Give God room to be God. It's OK if some things, even most things, don't make sense along the way.

A word of encouragement

The most encouraging thing to be said about our suffering is that, even in the most prolonged cases, it comes to an end. Paul put it far more eloquently: *"For our light affliction, which is but for a moment, is working for us a far more exceeding and eternal weight of glory, while we do not look at the things which are seen, but at the things which are not seen. For the things which are seen are temporary, but the things which are not seen are eternal"* (2 Cor. 4:17-18 NKJV).

18. Celebrate Good Things

A story to start

The loss of something of great value can lead one to despair, but the hope of its eventual recovery can keep you alive when it seems that nothing else matters. I am the father of a wayward son.

Shortly after daybreak, as I have done every day for months, I climbed the stairs to the roof and pulled my bench close to the low wall running around the edge. I started looking where I always look—at the place on the horizon where he disappeared. Though I don't really expect him to come back from that spot, that's where I always start. Nothing!

I scan to the right until I have taken in the full circle of the horizon. The sights where the earth touch the sky are like old friends now – a house with outbuildings, a small grove of olive trees, a meadow where the movement of the sheep there sometimes fool my old eyes, the rock strewn hill, the old fortress... I lean back, my careful scrutiny done, and focus on the middle distance taking in almost a full 180 degrees.

I wait. Every day I wait. Even when I am not here on the roof, I wait. Today, I will spend most of my time here. There is nothing more important to me. As the shadows change, I watch. Morning passes. A servant brings my mid-day meal of bread, dates, and fresh milk. I have much hope, but little expectation.

As I keep watch, I think. I plan. I remember my boy as a young child and weep to think of it. I still see my beloved Sarah's shining eyes as she presented him to me, his first steps, his silly infant charm, his roughhousing with his big brother, his pretending to work alongside the men, then a fiery youth carrying his own share of the labour. But in my mind, I don't just see pictures of the past. I see the future as clearly as a memory. I see my boy coming back. He will be walking slowly. He will be embarrassed. He always hated to admit it when he was wrong or mistaken.

As he comes to the edge of the barley field, I will get a good view of him and assure myself that the figure pausing there is not some passing stranger. As soon as I know it is him, I will go out to meet him. Sometimes, as I descend the stairs, I pretend to myself that I have seen him and practise taking two steps at a time.

Everything is prepared for his return. A robe hangs ready in the hallway. The servants know what it is for. I use it for my most honoured guests. It is the best robe in these parts, very fine, very costly.

In the niche in the wall where I keep my wax tablets and stylus, is a ring. It is engraved with my family's symbol, a barley sheaf with a plow to one side and a sickle on the other.

When he wears the robe he may feel like a guest, but when I put the ring on his finger, he'll know he's still part of the family. He'll know he's home.

A fat calf is penned nearby for the feast. Wine is laid away—sour, by now, of course—but mixed with honey and water, I'd serve it to the king. We'll have music, singing, dancing and stories.

Yes, everything is ready for his return. All we need to begin the celebration is the boy himself. That's why I'm up here on the roof today keeping watch. That's why you'll know where to find me every day until he finds his way home.

What are we talking about?

Celebration is a broad concept that has to do with observing or honouring a day, a person, an event, an achievement or a milestone. It is typically associated with positive emotions like happiness, joy and gladness. For Christians, celebration is part of worship. It begins with contemplating and appreciating who God is, then serves as a reminder of God's past faithfulness and stimulates our hope for anticipated blessing. When we think of His goodness in the past we can't stop our enthusiasm for Him from growing to the point of outward expression. Which leads me to one final comment. Celebration is about "getting it out there." Joy, gladness, happiness are all feelings. They need to be released physically. We celebrate to do that.

Biblical background

The idea of celebrating is thoroughly biblical. Examples of corporate, family and private celebration can be found throughout the Scriptures. Here are a few examples:

In Ezra 6:16 we read how the people of Israel, along with the Priests, the Levites, and the rest of the returned exiles, celebrated the dedication of the house of God with joy. Later, in the book which bears his name, we find Nehemiah's instructions to the people about how they were to celebrate: *"Go your way. Eat the fat and drink sweet wine and send portions to anyone who has nothing ready, for this day is holy to our Lord. And do not be grieved, for the joy of the LORD is your strength"* (Neh. 8:10 ESV). The usually gloomy prophet, Jeremiah, links celebration with vocal expressions, both singing and spoken word. *"Out of them shall come songs of thanksgiving, and the voices of those who celebrate. I will multiply them, and they shall not be few; I will make them honoured, and they shall not be small"* (Jer. 30:19 ESV).

> *"Go your way. Eat the fat and drink sweet wine and send portions to anyone who has nothing ready, for this day is holy to our Lord. And do not be grieved, for the joy of the LORD is your strength"* (Nehemiah 8:10 ESV)

In the familiar story of the prodigal son we read of the father's directions to his servants: *"'Bring quickly the best robe, and put it on him, and put a ring on his hand, and shoes on his feet. And bring the fattened calf and kill it, and let us eat and celebrate. For this my son was dead, and is alive again; he was lost, and is found.' And they began to celebrate"* (Luke 15:22-24 ESV).

The last one we'll look at doesn't use the word "celebrate" but the idea is clearly there. The words of the preacher: *"For everything there is a season, and a time for every matter under heaven: ... a time to weep, and a time to laugh; a time to mourn, and a time to dance"* (Eccl. 3:1... 4 ESV). While it's true that there is a time for weeping and mourning, it's also true that there is a time for laughing and dancing. That sounds a lot like celebration to me!

Exploring celebration

Robert Louis Stevenson, the Scottish author who lived from 1850-1894, wrote: "There is no duty we so much underrate as the duty of being happy."[1] Of all people, God's people have the most reason to celebrate.

Celebration helps us to...
...proclaim our satisfaction with God
...release our circumstances to God—reminding us of His sovereignty
...lighten the burdens of life
...remember the concept of Jubilee and the restoration of all things
...break the chains of an unrealistic understanding of success, hyper-productivity, and 24/7 availability
...remember that God wants us to enjoy Him and the life He gives us
...sense vitality in all aspects of the Christian life which could otherwise become drudgery

Taking cues from the world, many Christians think of celebration as legitimized over-indulgence. Gatherings of family and friends for seasonal holidays often feature a meal as the centre of the celebration. Abundance extends to the point of excess, but feasting need not be equated with excess. If we have more than we need, we can find less fortunate souls with whom to share the bounty and thus increase the celebration.

The activities or festivities associated with celebrating should never be allowed to overshadow what we are celebrating. Celebration is only significant when we keep in mind the reason for our engaging in it. Perhaps the best example is "celebrating" the Lord's supper.

Celebrate Good Things

Too often, people focus on the familiar ritual itself, as much as, or more than, on the act of remembering the Lord's victory over our sin at the cross.

Celebration proclaims our satisfaction with God. When we celebrate, we acknowledge God's ultimate redemptive power. That's why we can celebrate even in the worst of circumstances. We believe that God can redeem any situation for His glory and our good. Celebration releases our circumstances to God – reminding us of His sovereignty. When we celebrate, we let go of things and give them to God. This lightens the burdens of life.

> *Celebration is only significant when we keep in mind the reason for our engaging in it.*

We are responsible and accountable for our actions, but knowing that when our best ideas fail, and our best efforts are inadequate, and our best attempts at life often fall short of being our best, God is there to pick up the pieces and move us forward.

Celebration reminds us of the Old Testament concept of Jubilee. Deliverance, freedom and restoration are its great themes and powerful motivators to celebrate. Celebration also breaks the chains of hyper-productivity, 24/7 availability, and unrealistic concepts of success. Everything does not depend on us. We can give time to God and other people and still accomplish all we need to in life. This is really the only way to live. Taking time to celebrate reminds us that God wants us to enjoy Him and the life He gives us. Finally, I would like to suggest that celebration breathes vitality into all aspects of the Christian life which could otherwise become drudgery.

Practically, you can start looking for the things for which you can praise God, even in bad circumstances. I was amazed as I listened to my friend Dereje describe a home invasion which he experienced. He was systematically robbed of his meager possessions in a Kenyan refugee camp at gunpoint. When his assailants left, Dereje's first response was to slide off the bed where they had confined him onto his knees and praise God that He had spared His life. Only after celebrating God's goodness did he go out and rouse his neighbours to help him fix the damage the gunmen had done to his room.

To engage in authentic celebration we really have to know God. That includes knowing Him personally as well as knowing both what He has done for us and what He promises to do for us. Remember to exercise faith in God, not in some predetermined specific outcome. Those can disappoint. God never does. Stay open to the unexpected, the surprising, the creative ways of God. When you identify them, express gratitude. Share your joy with others. Exude hope. Live life at the optimistic end of the realism scale.

Potential pitfalls

The big danger with celebration is that it can become an end in itself. The expression of joy can be intoxicating and sweep us away with the process to the point that we lose sight of the object. Celebration should always point us to God, the giver of life, the redeemer of our souls, the provider of all good gifts, our only hope for eternity. I mention this, not to put a damper on the expression of our celebration, but to offer some perspective in a quiet moment so that we don't lose our way in the joy of the celebratory moment.

For some, there may be a hazard in celebration if we become unduly familiar with God and lose "the fear of the Lord." But if we celebrate appropriately, we won't fall into that trap because celebration always puts God in His proper place. We might say that it acts as insurance that our spiritual lives will have a healthy balance.

One last word of caution here: Remember that God didn't appoint you to police the celebration of your brothers and sisters.

A word of encouragement

Start looking for the brighter side of life instead of focussing on the heaviness and darkness which would oppress you. Laugh hard—at least once a day. Developing a healthy sense of humour takes us a long way in the right direction. Learn to enjoy the life God gives you without taking yourself too seriously. Read Paul's letter to the Philippians regularly, attempting to capture the spirit of joy expressed there for yourself. Lastly, get together with a few good friends and plan a celebration of God's goodness where you can all participate freely and enthusiastically.

---

1. Stevenson, Robert Louis—http://www.quotationspage.com/quote/37972.html

19. Rest

A story to start

To discover that you've been shaping your behaviour to conform to a false perception of the truth is unnerving. If you choose to live close to Jesus, you'd better be prepared to be unnerved... frequently. We thought we knew it all. We thought we knew God. We thought we knew the Law. We thought we knew how to do everything right. Then Jesus came. My name is James. As one of Jesus' inner circle of disciples I had a front row seat for things many only wish they could have seen.

One of the first things Jesus did after He began choosing his followers was to challenge the Pharisees. Every good-hearted Jew I knew was glad for this. We didn't know how they did it (or even if they did it), but we knew we couldn't come close to keeping the law as they taught it. Just seeing these men with their extra long tassels, their phylacteries firmly in place, their faces smug, made us almost want to do something illegal.

As followers of Jesus, we had to learn to get used to them, for they, too, decided to follow Jesus – but not because He chose them. They were keeping Jesus under observation because they detected a threat to their systems, both religious and political.

One day is particularly memorable. It was a Sabbath and the Master gave the word that we were going to visit the synagogue in Capernaum. He had just publicly proclaimed woe for that city because of the unbelief of the people, so we were curious about what His reception would be. We were a little ill prepared for the day's activities and most of us hadn't had anything to eat yet. Jesus decided to take a shortcut which led us beside a field of grain. I don't know who did it first, but a furtive hand shot out and grabbed a few heads of grain. Then another hand reached out... then another... As was His custom, Jesus kept turning to talk to us, so He saw what was going on, but made no negative comment.

Before long, we were all at it. We'd pause for a step, grab some grain, give it a rub in our hands to remove the chaff which we blew away with a quick puff, pop the grain into our mouths and walk along chewing it contentedly. We must have resembled a bunch of sheep following their shepherd. At the corner of the field, Jesus made a turn and, to our delight, we walked along another side of the field. This gave us more opportunity to fuel ourselves for the rest of the walk.

The Pharisees must have had spies watching us, for we had barely arrived at the end of the field when we saw a group of heavy men in billowing black cloaks approaching us. Some of us were still just nicely getting used to the constant adventure of being close to Jesus, so we were a little unsettled. Jesus, however, seemed to welcome their presence, aloof though they were.

They went on the offensive, challenging the Master because we were "threshing" on the Sabbath. Some of us felt bad because we had gotten Him into trouble. But He handled it without implicating us. He reminded them that David and his followers had eaten the holy bread in the house of God when they were hungry. He reminded them that the priests "worked" on the Sabbath as they carried out their duties. Then He turned everyone's thinking upside down by saying "The Sabbath was made for man, not man for the Sabbath."

That shut them up. We could see them mulling it over as they followed us to the synagogue. Jesus had taken the wind out of their sails temporarily, but they clearly weren't done with us yet.

What are we talking about?

Strictly speaking, rest is the cessation of labour. This rest need not demand absolute inactivity, though there is a place for that. We often speak of rest and relaxation together, suggesting that activities which are very different from those usually associated with the way we meet our physical needs is part of the "R and R" package. For our purposes, we will include relaxing activity along with inactivity as part of the rest which Christians should seek and practice.

Biblical background

We've already noted that God consecrated the seventh day for rest after having spent six days in creative activity (Gen. 2:2-3), but there are other passages which provide a biblical background for Sabbath rest. Sometimes it is viewed as a gift of God to be enjoyed: *"See! The LORD has given you the Sabbath; therefore on the sixth day he gives you bread for two days. Remain each of you in his place; let no one go out of his place on the seventh day. So the people rested on the seventh day"* (Ex. 16:29-30 ESV). Under the Mosaic law, the concept of Sabbath was framed as a command to be kept: *"Six days shall work be done, but on the seventh day is a Sabbath of solemn rest, a holy convocation. You shall do no work. It is a Sabbath to the LORD in all your dwelling places"* (Lev. 23:3 ESV).

Then, in Hebrews 4, we learn of a perpetual rest: *"So then, there remains a Sabbath rest for the people of God, for whoever has entered God's rest has also rested from his works as God did from his"* (Heb. 4:9-10 ESV).

Exploring rest

Work and rest have been associated from the beginning. The creation story ends with God devoting the seventh day to rest. The omnipotent Creator didn't need the rest, but by resting He set the pattern for us. Many people have a hard time resting. Keep in mind, I'm not talking just about sleeping, though sleep is included in rest. Rest is conscious inactivity, not mere unconsciousness. To be mentally alert while physically inactive allows us to rest at a level few reach. It creates a perfect environment for spiritual development as we can give undivided attention to God and what He is communicating to us.

Some think of "Sabbath" rather formally, but I believe that shortchanges God's intention. Sabbath rest, whether it is a full day a week or an hour or two a day, reminds us that we did not make the world, that we are not in charge, and that everything will not grind to a halt if we reduce our activity level. Sabbath is not a reward for us getting all of our work done. Rather than chafing at self-imposed restrictions which reduce our productivity, we can relax in our awareness that we trust God, not ourselves, to meet our needs.

> **Rest helps us to...**
> ...recuperate from the stress of work
> ...remember that God designed us to rest (we are not productivity machines)
> ...fulfill God's purpose for us

Because God initiated the concept of Sabbath rest at the very beginning, I conclude that He designed it because He knew we would need it when He designed us. Jesus highlighted this distinction when He said that the Sabbath was made for our sake not the other way round. (See Mark 2:27.) God did not create humans to have someone around to keep the Sabbath, rather he consecrated the Sabbath so humans would be able to get the rest they need to live healthy balanced lives. I also observe that the concept of Sabbath rest is found as early as the second chapter of Genesis, and though was built into the law, does not get all of its strength from the law. I believe that neglect of the Sabbath principle always has negative consequences.

Every day, our bodies remind us of our need for rest. In extreme cases, sleep will simply come upon us unbidden. We need to learn to rest before mind and body simply shut down. Rest allows us to recuperate from the stress of work. Our need for rest reminds us that God designed us to rest. We are not productivity machines. I would also suggest that rest fulfills some aspect of God's purpose for us.

I'm speaking from the "driven, hyper-productive" side of the fence and when I note some practical tips to get started, you'll see that right away. These thoughts reflect some challenges I confront. Try taking some time each week to engage in activities which are not designed to make money or to put food on the table. Once you've managed that, try blocking off some time to "do nothing." That's even harder. But remember the purpose of the exercise is not idleness. It is to allow your body, soul and spirit to recover from the constant use and sometimes abuse to which we subject them.

Potential pitfalls

Two potential pitfalls lie before us regarding rest. One is laziness. We can excuse sloth by calling it rest. For some, this may be a temptation. Others seem to be driven to the point where this will not be even remotely enticing. It is also possible to err as we practise "Sabbath rest" if we become legalistic about "certain" activities. We need not dig deep trenches where a simple line in the sand will do.

A word of encouragement

Many of the "rules" about the "Sabbath" were established during a time when "work" nearly always meant "physical labour." Consequently, doing anything that remotely resembled physical labour was seen as a violation of the Sabbath. Times are very different now. Many of us have sedentary jobs which, to the working class a century ago, would probably look like loafing. (After all, how hard can it be sitting at a desk pushing little buttons all day long?) But for people who do sit typing day after day, relaxation might take a more strenuous form, perhaps engaging in sports, splitting wood or doing some gardening.

Do whatever is necessary to shed a rule orientation to the Sabbath principle – resting as God did. Set time aside to do something that doesn't specifically contribute to your income to demonstrate that deep in your spirit, you recognize that God is the source of the things you need to live. He may provide you with work for pay which will allow you to meet your physical needs, but it is His provision, none-the-less. One last thought: Take a break from trying to be "in control" of your environment—especially the people in your environment – they need a break, too!

Our omnipotent God rested from His work and He wasn't even weary. How much more necessary and important is it for us to engage in this divine activity. As you move forward with God, remember that while we do benefit from rest physically and emotionally, the biggest benefit can be spiritual because our rest declares and illustrates our abiding confidence and trust in God.

Afterword

If you've read all, or even most, of this little book, I thank you. It was worth the effort. Before we part company, I'd like to remind you one last time of some of the many good reasons to pursue these *19 ways to boost your spiritual life*. You may want to refer to them again sometime to encourage yourself. By doing these things we...

1. follow Christ's example, expectations or commands
2. lessen the world's influence in our lives
3. consciously focus on God and the spiritual realm
4. develop concrete spiritual goals
5. direct our spiritual energy in physical ways
6. cooperate with God in our spiritual development
7. remind ourselves of our vulnerability

Along the way, I pointed out several specific potential dangers associated with certain activities, but there are general dangers that I would be so bold as to say always come with any attempt to walk more closely with God. The enemy hates our interest and effort in such things and will do what he can to discourage us. We also have our own sinful tendencies to deal with, so be on the alert. Some of the negatives associated with spiritual growth include:

1. The generation of spiritual pride
2. The development of a legalistic spirit
3. The development of a sense of entitlement
4. The very great likelihood of overt spiritual attack
5. The likelihood of new or intensified interpersonal conflict

If we are alert for these pitfalls, we can limit their effect and maximize the benefits of boosting out spiritual lives.

The Stories and Where to Find Them

1. Solitude—Gideon (Judges 6-8)
2. Silence—Elijah (1 Kings 19)
3. Confession—David (Psalm 51; 2 Samuel 11-12)
4. Meditation—Timothy (1 & 2 Timothy, especially 1 Timothy 4)
5. Service—Phoebe (Romans 16)
6. Prayer—Hezekiah (2 Kings 18-20; 2 Chronicles 28-33; Isaiah 36-39)
7. Fasting—Ezra (The whole book of Ezra, especially chapter 8)
8. Live Simply—John the Baptist (Early chapters of Matthew & Mark)
9. Sacrifice—Epaphroditus (Philippians esp. 2 and 4)
10. Generosity—Barnabas (Acts chapters 4 to 13)
11. Secrecy—Jonathan (1 Samuel 19)
12. Openness—Lydia (Acts 16)
13. Fellowship—John (his Gospel and Epistles)
14. Submission—Peter (Acts and 1&2 Peter)
15. Study—Nicodemus (John 3)
16. Worship—Solomon (2 Chronicles 3-8)
17. Suffering—Paul (2 Corinthians 11)
18. Celebrate—The Prodigal's Father (Luke 15:11-32)
19. Rest—James (Mark 2:23-28)

FBH International

Since its inception in 1951, this ministry has been all about the gospel. FBH International's central calling has been to radio ministry though it has had forays into print publishing and is now developing an internet presence. I have been serving with FBH International since the summer of 1993.

My personal conviction is that the gospel isn't just for unbelievers who need to hear it to be saved. That is where it all begins, to be sure, but believers need the gospel to touch their lives every day as well. If we come to think we've outgrown the need to apply the good news that Jesus died to bring us into a relationship with God, we've missed the thrust of Jesus' teaching – much of which revolved around how God's people should think, speak and act.

Consequently, FBH International has a two edged mission statement that incorporates communicating the gospel as the means through which Christians become conformed to His likeness as well as how unbelievers come to faith in the Lord Jesus Christ. We try to strike a balance between the two so that everyone within our reach is exposed to the gospel and then encouraged to grow in both knowledge and grace.

The material you've just read first came into being as a series of messages given at Elim Lodge (a Christian summer resort and retreat centre near Peterborough, Ontario, Canada). I reformatted the work I'd done into a series of features which we used on our radio program "Family Bible Hour" and articles on our website.

I've continued to add to the original work to this point so that now it is in book form for our international producers in English speaking areas to distribute as follow-up material to encourage their listeners in their spiritual development.

To learn more about this ministry and to find out how to join us in pursuing our vision to see people come to faith by hearing the word of God, visit **www.fbhinternational.com**.